D0968376

PRAISE FC
MORE NOW

"As the saying goes, 'children are our future.' This book is a comprehensive and insightful exploration of how to leverage our education systems to make that future as bright as possible. For educators yearning to transform their classrooms to parents hoping to tap into innovative ideas for their children, this book provides clear and practical ideas that will inspire action and hope in all of us.

"Education systems around the globe are exploring how to improve mindsets, systems, and practices to better prepare our students for the future. In this book, Dr. Mark Wagner compiles his vast experience with these systems, and his impressive network of educator colleagues within them, to weave a tapestry illustrating where we are today, where we can go tomorrow, and insightful suggestions for how we might get there."

—Jennie Magiera, author of *Courageous Edventures*

"*More Now* is the right book at the right time as we gain clarity and the courage to be architects of the future. Wagner does an elegant job of weaving his honeycomb framework and impressive impact experiences in a modern call to action for leaders in education, science, policy, and life in general. This is one of those books that will be dog eared and marked up as real leaders in real time will have the framework for real change! Thank you, Mark Wagner."

—Michael Lubelfeld, superintendent of schools,
coauthor of *The Unlearning Leader and Student Voice*

"Mark Wagner has always been light-years ahead when thinking about the future of education. This book does a great job of helping the rest of us catch up."

—Brendan Brennan, director of Moonshot Laboratory

"What a diverse cast of messages this book brings—as enjoyable and fast of a read as watching your favorite Netflix series. Each of the honeycomb elements and subsequent voices and messages builds on one another with inspirational energy and concrete ideas an educator needs to start or keep going with change. The further you read, the warmer the feeling gets inside you that you're not alone and that you're ready for the future with your students and colleagues."

—Wendy Gorton, educational technologist, author of *50 Hikes with Kids*

"*More Now* is more than a book. It is a gift to future generations of students in the world. It is a call to action for educators to think differently about what our students need now and what they will need in the future in order to be successful. This book will pull you out of your comfort zone and help you create the education that your students need and deserve."

—Dr. Nick Polyak, superintendent,
coauthor of *The Unlearning Leader and Student Voice*

"I highly recommend this book, as it is applicable to pre-service and in-service educators of all levels. If we want our students to embrace change and be prepared, we owe it to them to model this behavior by practicing it ourselves."

—Sarah Thomas, PhD, CEO and founder of EduMatch

"In *More Now: A Message from the Future for the Educators of Today*, Mark Wagner shows us an inspiring picture of what's possible for our schools. As an educator and a parent, this is a must-read that powerfully paves the educational pathways our children need."

—Trevor MacKenzie, author of *Dive into Inquiry* and *Inquiry Mindset*

"Mark Wagner describes the vibrant schools our students need today. He then draws on his extensive personal experience and global PLN to lay out a tangible roadmap that will make that vision a reality. Every educational leader should read this book."

—Mark Garrison, director of technology and innovation,
White Bear Lake Area Schools

"The future of humanity is in our learning spaces. What we do with this awesome responsibility determines what our future world will look like. Wagner addresses the hard reality that school change is never easy and that a one-size-fits-all solution to the complex cultural and organizational challenges does not exist. Instead, an integration of six impact elements map out the course to effective school change in order to provide "more now" to our learners.

"Dr. Wagner cleverly weaves relevant anecdotes, humor, and even pop culture as he takes his audience on a journey to the future in order to prepare students for their upcoming reality, now. His work addresses the needed changes through an achievable formula that is customizable to individual school needs.

"Education has always been about the future. In this masterful narrative, Dr. Mark Wagner connects education past to education future in order to address what our learning spaces can and should look like, now. This book outlines actionable steps for giving more to our students to prepare them for that future, and how we can do more as educators, now."

—Rachael Mann, coauthor of *The Martians in Your Classroom*

"Educators talk a lot about transforming schools, and yet we still don't seem to move forward as fast as we'd like. This book is a catalyst for the changes we all want to see in our schools. Read it and let's speed up the process."

—Heather Dowd, dynamic learning project mentor,
coauthor of *Classroom Management in the Digital Age*

"Until the crew at The Moonshot Factory finish their secret work on a flux capacitor, this book is the best way to get a glimpse of where we're headed and where our students need to be. Mark has always been a visionary, and with *More Now*, we can have a look through his optimistic and inspiring point of view."

—Kevin Brookhouser, author of *20% Time* and *Code in Every Classroom*

"Mark is one of those brave souls who has climbed the beanstalk to stand on the shoulder of giants in order to show us the view of what education is, what it should be, and what the possibilities are for the future. If there was ever a voice from the future that was reaching out to the present-day educator in the hopes of making the possibilities of tomorrow the realities of today, *More Now* is the manual to help us reach our potential. *More Now* provides a roadmap to help anyone trapped in the current, and ancient, industrial-era education system we currently use, reach out and revolutionize his or her pedagogy. When the caterpillar asked Alice, 'Who are you?' she responded, 'I know who I was when I got up this morning. But I think I must have been changed several times since then.' If you're lucky this will be how you feel after reading this book."

—John Wick, EdD, director of education, Qneuro

Mark Wagner, PhD

MORE NOW

A Message from the **Future**
for the **Educators** of Today

More Now
© 2018 by Mark Wagner, PhD

All rights reserved. No part of this publication may be reproduced in any form or by any electronic or mechanical means, including information storage and retrieval systems, without permission in writing by the publisher, except by a reviewer who may quote brief passages in a review. For information regarding permission, contact the publisher at press@edtechteam.com.

These books are available at special discounts when purchased in quantity for use as premiums, promotions, fundraising and educational use. For inquiries and details, contact the publisher: edtechteam.com/press.

Published by EdTechTeam Press
Cover Design by Genesis Kohler
Cover photo by MaynRad Brenes
Editing and Layout by My Writers' Connection

Library of Congress Control Number: 2018945812
Paperback ISBN: 978-1-945167-49-2
eBook ISBN: 978-1-945167-50-8

Irvine, California

To every educator who accepts the past,
loves their students in the present,
and works every day to make a better future.

This is only the beginning.

CONTENTS

FOREWORD 11

1 THERE IS NO LIMIT 15

2 COURAGEOUS LEADERS 33

3 EMPOWERED TEACHERS 55

4 STUDENT AGENCY 73

5 INSPIRING SPACES 95

6 ROBUST INFRASTRUCTURE 109

7 ENGAGED COMMUNITY 127

8 MORE *NOW* 141

EDTECHTEAM VALUES 157

BIBLIOGRAPHY 163

ACKNOWLEDGMENTS 165

ABOUT THE AUTHOR 173

FOREWORD

by Karen Cator, CEO of Digital Promise

Technology is changing how we live and work. Similarly, technology is changing how we learn. This should surprise no one.

Seventy-seven percent of Americans now own smartphones and use them to instantaneously communicate with virtually anyone in the world, search and find information and resources on any topic, access or purchase any available product or service, and create and share content with the world. With technologies such as artificial intelligence, machine learning, and robotics, we can also automate numerous services and activities, from cashiering in a fast food restaurant to opening a bank account to assisting physicians in diagnosing diseases. The massive amounts of data we can collect and analyze give us the ability to see the world, and its opportunities and problems, in new ways and on a scale never before possible.

In short, technology continues to reshape economic and daily life, disrupting business practices and everyday social norms.

Not all of technology's influences are positive. We are living in what some observers call the post-truth era, where "fake news" and "alternative facts" are often indistinguishable from vetted information from trusted sources. Foreign governments are taking advantage of our confusion to undermine our democracy. As technology becomes even more deeply embedded in our daily lives, thought-provoking questions educators have always asked themselves are now essential:

Which skills and competencies will young people need to not only survive but thrive in a technology-driven world?

How do we think about educating the next generation to be able to tell the difference between fact and propaganda?

What can we do to ensure technology makes a positive contribution to the evolution of a more productive, inclusive, and equitable education system?

One thing is clear: all young Americans should become familiar with and adept at using and understanding technology, data, and information.

So, where do we start?

As Mark Wagner writes in this book, "School change is never easy, and there is no single 'right' answer to the complex cultural and organizational challenges ahead."

One answer, however, lies in making sure that, even as we use technology to improve education, we maintain a relentless focus on people—and especially relationships between teachers and students, education leaders and teachers, leaders and policymakers, students and other students, their parents, and communities.

For all its power and pervasiveness, technology is not a replacement for teachers—and it shouldn't be. Many of the highly complex and nuanced demands of teaching and learning cannot be met by computers executing instructions or even sophisticated, self-learning algorithms seemingly working without human guidance. People learn in different ways, at different rates—and diverse variables can affect their progression on any given day, including those in the social and emotional realm.

Then, there are those serendipitous moments, when students become captivated by an activity, a current event, or a challenge and engage with an intensity that could not have been foreseen. The best teachers harness this energy and use it as rocket fuel for learning.

This does not mean technology has not changed the role of the teacher. It has—and dramatically. In schools and classrooms all over the country, ubiquitous access to technology has given motivated teachers the chance to shift from being deliverers of content to what many have dubbed orchestrators of learning. They study advances in the learning sciences to better understand how people learn. They personalize learning for each student, using data from learning technologies available in the classroom. And they listen, observe, engage, motivate, group, and regroup students to provide optimal learning opportunities for each and all.

For positive change to occur in our schools, education stakeholders must work together to envision the future, develop a roadmap, innovate everywhere, and act with appropriate speed. I am reminded of Marshall McLuhan's quote about the future: "We look at the present through a rear-view mirror. We march backwards into the future."

This is a timely and insightful book that will help educators embrace the principles of reinvention—even when we can't always see where we're going.

Thank you, Mark, for providing this clear perspective, pulling together these voices and stories, and sharing your model for school change with a broader audience!

CHAPTER ONE
THERE IS NO LIMIT

Solving big problems is easier than
solving little problems.
—**Sergey Brin, cofounder of Google**

If you don't already, you should know that I'm a fan of the Irish rock band U2. I often find that the themes of their songs and performances resonate with me as an educator, and I draw a lot of inspiration from their lyrics when preparing professional development experiences. Often, I'll begin a presentation or workshop with an anecdote about the band, and it may be best to begin this book that way too. If nothing else, perhaps it will help me connect with you on a more human level—even through the pages of a book.

In any case, during the first two legs of U2's Vertigo Tour in 2005, the band played their new song "Miracle Drug" at every concert. The inspiration behind this anthemic rock song's lyrics really hit home with me as both a parent and an educator, and it has stuck with me to this day.

As the story goes, a boy named Christopher Nolan showed up at Mount Temple Comprehensive School, in Dublin, Ireland, at the same time as Bono and the other band members. Complications during birth had deprived Nolan's brain of oxygen and resulted in his being born with

Hear Bono share the inspiring story behind "Miracle Drug" from the stage.

cerebral palsy. He had no use of his voluntary muscles, and doctors had no reason to believe Nolan had any significant brain activity. His parents, however, refused to give up on him. They believed he could understand what was going on, and they included him in their lives. They took him places, read to him, and spoke to him constantly. When Nolan was ten years old, scientists developed what his parents thought of as a miracle drug, thus the title of the song. The drug relaxed his body enough to give him limited use of his neck. Now, moving your neck while still being completely confined by your body may not sound like much of a miracle, but for Christopher Nolan, it changed everything. Wearing a pointer on his head, he was able to type—able to communicate with the world for the first time in his life. The words came tumbling out, and by the age of fifteen, Nolan's first book, *Dam-Burst of Dreams*, was published. He continued writing and became a well-known novelist in Ireland. Nolan's story inspired the lyrics of "Miracle Drug" and shines a light on the unlimited potential that exists in the relationship between science and humanity:

> **Of science and the human heart**
> **There is no limit.**

The song speaks to me because I see this truth played out every day in the work I am privileged to be part of with EdTechTeam as we help educators around the world bring technology into classrooms. When we marry the power of technology with the heart of a teacher, there is no limit to what our students can create or achieve. And like Nolan's parents, we can never give up on them.

You Are an Architect of What's Possible

I'm a former high school English teacher, and I've had the good fortune to be an education technology coordinator at the school, district, and county levels. About ten years ago, I left my job at the county office and founded EdTechTeam. It's something of a dream job for me, getting to work with an amazing team and inspiring educators around the globe.

During the past few years, I have visited schools all over the world and have had the opportunity to learn from forward-thinking educators. The innovative learning environments they create give us a glimpse of the future, and more importantly, of the possibilities that exist for students today. Each year, EdTechTeam hosts more than 500 face-to-face and online events attended by almost 100,000 educators—educators who, like you, dream big and want to explore what's possible.

That's what this book is designed to help you do: to help raise your awareness regarding what's possible today, to inspire you to develop your own vision for the future, and to empower you to take the next steps yourself. We'll look at what's working in schools today and at how educators at all levels are striving to expand possibilities for those within their school communities.

Being an advocate for technology in education, I continually hear about cutting-edge technology. A few years ago, I had the opportunity to try Google Glass when it hit the public market. To be honest, I was initially ambivalent. The concept of a hands-free device that allowed people to actively participate in life while using it (rather than staring down at their devices all day) sounded great, but I wasn't sure that the $1,500 price tag would be well-spent money. I wasn't sure, that is, until I received the box in the mail. Inside, along with the high-tech glasses, was a little piece of paper with these words on it:

"You are a pioneer, a founder, and an architect of what's possible."

Whatever you think about Google Glass and its subsequent iterations, I felt a tremendous sense of excitement about being an _architect of the possible_ when I put on those glasses. It's the same sense of excitement I feel about our work as educators and educational technologists. Google is no stranger to being an architect of the possible, and, like other future-focused tech companies such as Apple, Qneuro, and others we'll talk about in this book, Google isn't afraid to attack problems and seemingly

"What is Moonshot Thinking?"
X's promo video

impossible ideas as they build our future for us. At X, Google's semi-secret research-and-development, "moonshot" laboratory, tech pioneers identify huge problems, dream up "radical solutions," and apply (or create) breakthrough technology to solve those problems.

That is the core of *moonshot thinking*: being willing to go beyond what has been previously imagined and finding solutions and new ways of doing things that take us further than we've ever been. The phrase *moonshot thinking* alludes to President John F. Kennedy's inspiring speech that pushed the United States to put a man on the Moon, an idea that previously seemed improbable if not impossible. At X, you can see moonshot thinking in action with Project Loon, which transmits high-speed internet via balloons in the stratosphere to bring connectivity to the world's remotest areas. Another project, Waymo, is a self-driving car. Waymo has "graduated" from X, and the cars are being used in the real world, where they have the potential to reduce accidents and commute frustrations while making it easy for those who can't drive to get where they need to go.

In his 2013 TED Talk, Google President Sergey Brin noted that the problem addressed by the Google Glass project (or one of them, anyway) was the fact that for all the convenience we enjoy with smartphones and other personal-technology devices, too often we end up disconnecting from the people around us every time we look down at our phones. For me, this *Minority Report* kind of tech brought the future into view, and I didn't have to disengage from the world around me to enjoy it. I could see more and experience more, *now*. And that's really the point of education technology: to provide powerful opportunities to engage our students, to connect them with the future—and with one another and the world—right now.

Fortunately, not all tech comes with a huge price tag. Google Cardboard's creators didn't initially envision making a big impact on education, but with a few dollars' worth of cardboard wrapped around a smartphone, the app gives users an immersive virtual reality (VR) experience. On its own, the novelty of VR is exciting, but it turns out that when you put a team of educators and engineers together and give them affordable and accessible VR technology, they'll create something even more amazing.

Pairing Google Cardboard, existing Street View imagery, and an amazing and growing library of imagery, a team of educators and engineers built the Google Expeditions app, which takes students on virtual field trips to exotic locations all over the world—places to which you never could take a field trip in a bus, including the planet Mars—without ever leaving the classroom. As we finished the final draft of this book, Google just released the Tour Creator so teachers and students can create their own expeditions. And the week previous, Facebook released the Oculus Go, a stand-alone VR headset (with a hand-held controller for additional interaction—and with no need to connect it to a PC or phone). I'm sure there'll be more to come out of these innovations (or whatever iterations come next) as more teachers and students learn to create their own unique VR experiences.

Imagining What's Possible for Schools

At EdTechTeam, our mission is to inspire and empower educators to effect school change using the best learning principles and technology available. We want to stimulate the kind of moonshot thinking that we see happening at Google and with the educators who helped craft Google Expeditions. We know that when students, teachers, and education leaders dream big and find ways to apply technology to learning, they change the way we *all* learn and interact with the world. Even as tech companies shape the way we experience the world, empowered educators and innovative students have the power to create the future.

The trouble is that it can be difficult to imagine new possibilities when we're so familiar with the challenges and problems facing education today. When people work in any field for the magical 10,000 hours required for mastery (which happens to be about five to six years into a typical career), they learn the problems in their field; they get a feel for how things naturally develop and transpire. That experience trains people to make habitual, reactive, and preemptive decisions. It's much easier to make assumptions that something new won't work. For as much as experience supports an educator's work in so many ways, experience can also cause us to completely miss opportunities to make subtle or even major shifts in education.

> **Empowered educators and innovative students have the power to create the future.**

Part of our job at EdTechTeam is to disrupt that tendency to shift into autopilot. Rather than simply acting on developed instincts, the challenge we set before educators—before you—is to drop preconceptions. Our goal is to raise awareness of what's possible, to help you enjoy and act on the excitement you feel for your unique vision, and to empower you with confidence so you can move forward and fulfill *your* goals. So, while considering the problems facing schools today, I hope you'll be open to inspiration and to imagining radical solutions, and then take the first step, however small, toward better learning

School change is never easy, and there is no single "right" answer to the complex cultural and organizational challenges ahead. What we've learned from forward-thinking schools around the globe, however, is that there are six elements that are essential for creating schools where educators and students can dream big and reach their goals. These may look different at different schools, but we find the schools that are having the biggest impact are all doing especially well in each of these areas: **courageous leaders, empowered teachers, student agency, inspiring spaces, robust infrastructure,** and an **engaged community**.

We call this the honeycomb of school change , and it provides a visual representation and interactive map for implementing positive school change. By integrating the six elements of the honeycomb, schools can equip and empower students to thrive and make an impact on the world around them *starting now*. Throughout the rest of this book, we'll travel around the honeycomb, learning (from teachers as well as education and tech-industry leaders) about what some of today's best schools are doing to ensure their students are indeed ready for their future. Before we dive in, I want to give you a overview of each of the six areas we'll be exploring.

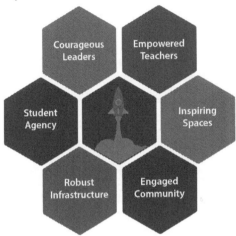

Courageous Leaders

Courageous leaders are connected, collaborative, and visionary risk takers who support initiative and innovation in others.

Courageous leaders hold a place at the top of the list because leadership affects every aspect of a school. That truth came into sharp focus for me when we started hosting EdTechTeam summits at amazing schools all over the world. What we realized was, regardless of the country, the system of education, the focus of the school, or the number of computers they had, one of the things that made all of those schools special was the leadership that hosted us.

It wasn't a coincidence that we wound up at schools with visionary leaders; those leaders hosted the events *because* they wanted to provide powerful professional learning experiences for their teachers and engaging opportunities for their students. But as we got to know these leaders, we realized that they all had different agendas, biases, and focuses. They all bucked tradition and took risks to make things happen at their schools, and they accepted responsibility for the results in their buildings or districts regardless of what their peers, or even those further up the chain of command, were telling them. To make their vision of student success come to life, they intentionally connected and collaborated with their teams, peers, other leaders, and their school communities.

Empowered Teachers

Empowered teachers are passionate educators with the tools, professional development, and time to create engaging experiences for students.

Passion is an essential characteristic of an empowered teacher; it is something the teacher must bring into his or her work. Most educators are innately passionate about helping kids and about making the future better for them. Unless they're totally burned out, they bring that passion with them to work each day. What teachers often lack, however, are the tools, training, and time they need to create engaging experiences for students.

Over and over again, we've seen that the most innovative schools place a priority on providing teachers powerful professional development opportunities. Their leaders dedicate time for professional learning as well as funds for training and tools, and then they give teachers the space, hours, and freedom to explore, try, and even fail forward as they test and implement new methods and strategies.

The New Zealand school system provides one of the best examples of empowered teachers I've seen. Richard Wells, deputy principal for a high school in New Zealand and the author of *A Learner's Paradise*, says he believes that trust is another crucial component for creating a culture in which teachers feel confident and empowered. Twenty years ago, the New Zealand government gave up control of the responsibility for establishing

GUEST VOICE: RICHARD WELLS
ADAPT, STARTING NOW

Deputy Principal, @eduwells, EduWells.com,

Auckland, New Zealand

If you want to do any big national change to your education system, it's going to take twenty years before things become the norm. So you have to start today, and you have to get everybody into the mindset of adapting to the world's current and future demands. What the world values now is different from what it valued fifteen years ago, and we must grade and measure accordingly.

Adapting in education comes down to being observant of the life that you lead. In my job as a deputy principal in a school, for example, I'm not allowed to use a pen to handwrite a message or letter or parent letter; it must be delivered via secure, digital communication. We live in a world that doesn't allow the pen! It's difficult, then, to make the argument for handwriting these days. In terms of adaptation, teachers who argue for old methods and for holding to those things we used to value highly are just not observant of their own behavior.

A Message from the Future

Adapt and open your eyes because the future is right in front of you; you've just got to look at what's going on.

learning outcomes, and handed off this power to the local schools and teachers. Wells describes the autonomous system by which the schools operate today as a "high-trust model," where teachers are empowered to design learning opportunities and assessments *with* the students. "Teachers tailor and personalize learning to meet their students' needs and the needs of community," Wells explains. The result has been a move toward an environment where, he says, "the individual students have control over the way they go about learning."

When we track the evolution of New Zealand's education system, it's easy to see how courageous leadership (demonstrated by government-level leaders handing over control to those closest to the learning) empowers teachers to create engaging learning experiences for students. And as Wells notes, one of the outcomes is student agency, which happens to be the next element in the honeycomb—and perhaps the most important.

Student Agency

Student agency is a focus on helping students find, organize, and use information to create, collaborate, and share in ways that are meaningful to them and to others in the outside world.

Students are capable of solving real-world problems. When we empower them to tap into that potential while they're still in school, they learn that they have the ability (and perhaps even the responsibility) to make a difference in the world.

If you took a tour of New Zealand's Albany Senior High School and listened in on the students' conversations as they work, you might hear them discussing the software, sustainable energy sources, or cars they're creating. When I met with Mark Osborne in 2012, he was serving as the assistant principal of Albany Senior High. In that role, he occasionally offered tours of the campus and would frequently play a game he called "Where's the teacher?" As students worked in groups in the school's open and flexible spaces, it was difficult for visitors to tell who the teacher was.

If visitors could win the game, Osborne said, the teachers were doing something wrong.

At Albany, students own and lead their learning while teachers work alongside them rather than standing at the front of the room. Student agency is baked right into everything this school does. Adopting the powerful concept of "20 percent time," the leadership at this school allots students one full day a week to work on what they call "Impact Projects." Every Wednesday, all day, all students work on their projects.

Students present proposals for their projects to three staff members and, once their ideas are approved, they're off to the races. The campus is rich with evidence of student-driven learning, such as murals painted by the students, a windmill that generates renewable energy, and a sustainable garden that produces organic food. Students also write plays, produce movies, create software, build cars, and pursue other passions as varied as the students are.

When schools promote student agency, kids get engaged with learning in ways that traditional lesson plans just can't match. They get excited regarding the learning in part because they care about and are interested in the topics they're studying. More than that, they often get involved in projects that make a real impact on their schools, communities, and around the world. They learn that they have a voice and the power to use it to make a difference.

Inspiring Spaces

Inspiring spaces are comfortable, beautiful, and flexible environments that invite students to learn by engaging their curiosity, wonder, and natural physical energy.

Learning spaces should reflect the culture of learning at the school. One of the things we have noticed about the schools that impressed us the most—schools where the focus is clearly on student agency rather than adult authority—is that they don't look like ordinary schools. Rather than classrooms with traditional desks lined up in rows where teachers lecture from the front of a room, the spaces and furniture in schools like Albany Senior High School are flexible.

There, students gather in open learning areas divided by rolling whiteboards. They push furniture around to suit their purposes, whether that's to collaborate with a few other students or brainstorm and test ideas in large groups. And as you'll learn in Chapter Five from Rebecca Hare, coauthor of *The Space*, creating these inspiring spaces doesn't require a huge budget. Simple changes can contribute in huge ways to student agency and engagement.

Robust Infrastructure

Robust infrastructure comprises the technology, networks, hardware, and other resources (including policy) that make deeper experiences possible— without detracting from the learning.

"We need to take the best of what education is, think about where technology plays a role, and then use it to bring education to the next level," says Jaime Casap, chief education evangelist at Google. At EdTechTeam, we believe the technology and infrastructure in a school should support courageous leaders, empowered teachers, a student-agency focus, and the creation and operation of inspiring spaces. We don't advocate for bringing computers into the classroom because we want to make life harder for the IT department. We bring technology into the classroom as a means of supporting all of the other elements of the honeycomb, especially student agency. Whether you work in a 1:1 school with Wi-Fi throughout, have computer carts that move from class to class, or share a single computer in your classroom or department, the infrastructure makes it possible—or impossible—to use. If you've ever had a lesson waylaid by a video or image that wouldn't load or a video call that couldn't connect, you know that technology has to work when you need it. The platforms and programs in your school need to be seamless so that students and staff members are empowered rather than frustrated by those tools and systems. A robust

GUEST VOICE: JAIME CASAP
OVERCOMING OBJECTIONS

Chief Education Evangelist, Google, @jcasap,

Phoenix, Arizona

One of the questions I get all the time when I do Q&A is, "How do you deal with resistance to change?" Sometimes it's parents who don't want things to change; they're used to school being a certain way. So I think it's absolutely critical to engage parents, for example, to tell them that you're preparing kids for the future. Relate the changes to the way they're experiencing life today. Ask parents, "What was your grade last year for your performance? Oh, and by the way, I assume that in your office, everyone you work with is the same age as you, right?" Of course, it's ridiculous, but it helps tie in to the way they work in the real world, and it allows them to start seeing that these models we're trying to implement make sense.

We're not preparing kids for that old world; we're preparing them for the world that their parents are already in today.

A Message from the Future

I think what we need in education is to eliminate this idea that we're building toward something, because we're not. We're building a future of continuous innovation and iteration. We're constantly getting better at what we do, and we're reflecting the world that we face, and ironically or not, that's exactly what the future is. The future is about iteration and innovation.

infrastructure, including relevant policies, ensures that whatever technology you have access to supports—rather than detracts from—learning.

Engaged Community

Engaged community members understand what is possible in schools today, are included in the school vision, and are active in partnerships with the school.

When we refer to an engaged community, we're talking about the school's community of parents and other family members as well as those who may have no direct affiliation with the school. Local business owners, government leaders, and members of the media should all be considered as part of a school's community.

If you're wondering why it matters if the people in your town or city know about your school, consider what happens when you propose investing money to build robust infrastructure or design flexible learning spaces. Very often, the community has a vote and financial stake in what happens in schools. Sometimes, they are the very people who approve, deny, or donate the funds, resources, or time necessary to make your vision for your school a reality. If you've communicated your vision well and your community understands the potential impact of that vision, it's possible to eliminate some of the most common challenges schools face when proposing initiatives that require funding, updated technology policies, or revised testing and assessment measures. Rather than being an obstacle to get around, an engaged community can provide the support (or drive) you need to make things happen.

As you think about your needs or concerns regarding the different elements of school change, you may want to jump to a particular section of the honeycomb. That's great, but I do encourage you to come back and read from beginning to end; I think you'll be inspired by the educators and schools whose stories are shared in each chapter.

A Message from the Future

At a U2 concert in Toronto (one I saw recorded rather than live, sadly), The Edge's opening riffs to "Miracle Drug" made Bono pause. Looking to the audience, Bono explained the notes were actually the sound The Edge's spaceship made when he came to Earth. (Edge is a bit of a geek, and the band likes to joke that he's from another planet.) Then Bono said, "Myself [sic], Adam, and Larry were at school on the Northside of Dublin, and we saw this spaceship and it was playing this sound, even back then, and the spaceship landed, and The Edge got out.

"And we said, 'Where are you from?'

"And The Edge said, 'I'm from the future.'

"And Larry said, 'What's it like?'

"And Edge said, *It's better!*'"

Those words, like the song itself, spoke to me. The dream of creating a better future for education—starting now—is the driving theme of this book. And because you're reading it, my guess is that you share that dream and belief that there is a better future for our kids and that bringing technologies and new pedagogies into the classroom is going to create a better future for all of us.

You are an architect of the possible.

As we dive into each of the six areas of the honeycomb and learn together what our peers and leaders are doing, I want to remind you of this thought: *You are an architect of the possible.* The opportunities you create for your learners (teachers or students) will help them shape a better future for themselves—and for the world. And as we work together to bring the best technology and best pedagogy into classrooms, we are creating learning opportunities that prepare today's students for tomorrow's world.

GUEST VOICE: RICHARD CULATTA
EQUITY AND ACCESS FOR ALL

CEO at International Society for Technology in Education, @rec54,
Washington, DC

One of the biggest challenges in education today is the huge disparities between different groups of people in our system. That's not news to anybody, but it feels like we've been admiring the problem for too long and really need to be thinking more creatively and finding ways to close long-standing equity gaps. It strikes me that technology brings to the table a whole set of tools that we have not had before.

It's not necessarily that the tech is all new, but until recently we really haven't had access in schools at a level that you could actually take advantage of these new tech solutions. We're finally getting to that point. Do we still need to improve connectivity? Of course. Are there still schools that don't have the connectivity or kids at home that don't have the connectivity that they need? Of course. But by and large, we're at a place where the infrastructure has caught up to a point that we can start to look at bringing these tech tools to bear on this very long-standing problem of inequity.

And I believe technology is the most powerful tool we have to close persistent equity gaps in education, if we choose to use it that way. We have a window of opportunity to determine and set the pattern for the use of technology to tackle tough issues of equity. And unfortunately, that window is not a very big one. We're at an inflection point. And the question is, how do we actually rethink the role of education and redesign education around these new tools that are being afforded to us?

> We have a window of opportunity to determine and set the pattern for the use of technology to tackle tough issues of equity. And unfortunately, that window is not a very big one.

There are two major considerations when you're looking at using technology to transform learning. One is you have to have infrastructure in place. The second is that you have to have teachers who are prepared to use it effectively. Fortunately, we have passed the tipping point on the infrastructure. Where we need massive amounts of additional focus is on preparing teachers to use that technology effectively. That's the difference that I see in schools that are doing it well versus ones that are struggling.

A Message from the Future

Step it up a bit. Every day that goes by in which students aren't receiving learning experiences that are tailored to their needs is one more day where we lose students. We're going to get there. It's not a question of whether we will or not; I'm convinced that we'll get there. But how long do we have to wait while we continue to lose students?

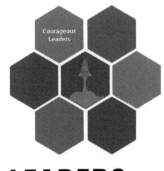

CHAPTER TWO
COURAGEOUS LEADERS

If your actions inspire others to dream more,
learn more, do more, and become more,
you are a leader.
–John Quincy Adams

Courageous leaders are connected, collaborative, and visionary risk takers who support initiative and innovation in others.

Courageous leaders have the power to change the world. When President Kennedy gave his famous moonshot speech in 1961, he didn't have any idea how the United States was going to put someone on the Moon. The technology needed to complete the mission hadn't been invented yet. But he had a clear vision: The United States was going to the Moon. Kennedy believed that the nation could attain that seemingly impossible goal because he understood the unlimited potential that is unleashed when humans combine imagination, innovation, and focused effort with a spirit of determination.

I believe we possess all the resources and talents necessary. But the facts of the matter are that we have never made the national decisions or marshaled the national resources required for such leadership. We have never specified long-range goals on an urgent time schedule, or managed our resources and our time so as to ensure their fulfillment.
–President John F. Kennedy

It's with this same determined spirit that Polynesian islanders climbed into dugout canoes and headed toward the horizon. They didn't know what they would find, but with a courageous spirit of adventure and exploration, they migrated and populated one thousand islands five hundred years before Columbus arrived in North America. This daring and persistent spirit that looks to the unknown and aims for the Moon or aims for one of a thousand unseen islands—not knowing how you're going to get there—is what leaders in education need today.

Schools are desperate for leaders who will set a long-range vision, complete with an urgent time schedule, and who will commit the energy and resources to ensure its fulfillment. Being a courageous leader means that you're willing to think beyond today's crisis or this year's test scores. It means being willing to design a school or system that serves today's learners in a way that prepares them for their future.

The courageous leaders I've met are not afraid to buck tradition. They allow their educators and students to dream big and take risks. They work hard to empower their teachers, to create inspiring spaces for learning, and to make sure their schools are equipped with the resources and robust infrastructure that make it possible for all students to have engaging and personalized educational experiences. They look beyond their school and office walls to connect and collaborate with other educators in their building and around the world to see what's possible for today's students. They strive to gain the support of their communities by making sure to communicate what's happening—and how things could be even better—within their schools. In short, the courageous leaders I've met—district leaders, building-level leaders, or teacher-leaders—have a vision of doing something awesome for their schools, and they are willing to do whatever it takes to see its fruition.

What's Your Moonshot?

When I'm working with educators in our Moonshot Thinking workshops, I always ask: "What big, meaningful problem do you want to solve?" In other words, what's your moonshot? Some start with modest goals like "improve attendance." Some are more ambitious and want to create a school with "no grades" or "20% time all the time." Very few aspire to something world changing that transcends education, like "solve racism."

It's easy for school leaders to get stuck working on little problems, dealing with day-to-day emergencies, and trying to manage everything and everyone. But the job of the courageous leader is to be the architect of the possible, something that requires making time and space to focus on the big, meaningful problems that need to be solved. So, what's your moonshot? Take a few moments to write down a few of the meaningful problems that may be preventing your district, school, or classroom from reaching its potential. And whatever you're thinking . . . think bigger. You can always think big, but start small, after all. (Use the space provided on the next page. Once you've made your list, circle just one problem to focus on for this exercise.)

When innovators at X begin a new project, this is how they get started: by identifying a problem. Once you know where to focus your energy, you can move to the next step: ideation or brainstorming ideas to solve the problem. But let me encourage you *not* to start by listing the easiest or most sensible or probable solutions. Begin by listing what you *wish* could happen, even if those solutions seem impossible or improbable. Even if the ideas are way out there, that's okay. The point of this exercise is to get your creative juices flowing. Even the most outlandish ideas can spark insight that leads to an innovative solution. With your big, meaningful problem in mind, take two minutes right now to list as many solutions as you can think of. Write them down even if they seem completely far-fetched or impossible.

Come back to this space over the next few days, and continue adding to the list of ideas. Among them, you just may find the solution—or a primitive variation of the solution.

What big, meaningful problems do you want to solve?

(List as many as you can think of, then circle one to focus on.)

Use this space to brainstorm solutions.

(Don't limit possible solutions to reality!)

Here's just one example of how this has worked for other educators. Truancy and skipping classes is a fairly common problem in many high schools. During one school's brainstorming session that focused on how to solve the problem of students walking off campus, someone jokingly suggested a shock collar for students that would zap students when they left campus during school hours—a completely unrealistic and inhumane idea. But out of that idea came a plan to create an app that would notify students and parents when the kids left the school grounds without permission. What started as an outlandish idea turned into a realistic potential solution for reducing truancy.

Applying Google's Pillars of Innovation to Your Vision for School Change

A blog post by Susan Wojcicki inspired Sylvia Duckworth to create the sketchnote above. When she wrote the piece, Wojcicki was the vice president of advertising for Google. Today, she's the CEO of YouTube. To say she knows a thing or two concerning innovation is an understatement. The concepts she highlights as the foundation of Google's culture of innovation are simple and profound. They also tend to resonate with educators, particularly those who are courageous enough to tackle the big problems. As you move through the other areas of the honeycomb, you'll see these eight essentials of innovation resurface.

1. Have a mission that matters. Google's mission is to "organize the world's information and make it universally accessible and useful." That statement acts as both a filter and a lens—sifting out ideas that didn't fit or apply and bringing the ideas that needed attention into sharp focus. Our mission as educators is very similar to Google's. It is to help students access and use information. Our job is no longer to help students memorize a few things they might need someday. Everything you do, including the effort you'll put into solving that big, meaningful problem you identified earlier, needs to support that mission of equipping learners to access, understand, and use information so they can use it to change the world.

2. Think big, but start small. Your big idea may seem overwhelming or even impossible to accomplish. Then again, the idea of a self-driving car seems a little far-fetched. The important thing here is to think big but start small. James Sanders wanted to change education and offer millions of students something different (and more engaging) when he launched Breakout EDU, an educational gaming platform that brings the fun and challenge of an escape room into schools. But Sanders didn't start with a million-dollar operation. He started by buying locks and parts at a hardware store, putting together one kit (in a toolbox he spray painted), and then testing it with real teachers at an EdTechTeam summit within thirty days after coming up with the idea—and then with students thirty days later. Every major innovation starts with small steps of progress toward the ultimate goal. What small steps can you take toward the outcome you desire?

3. Strive for continual improvement. Chris Lehmann, the founding principal and CEO of the Science Leadership Academy network of schools, believes that problems aren't necessarily solved with huge sweeping changes but through incremental improvements. Constant iterations and small tweaks can lead to massive progress over time. As Wojcicki explains,

"Our iterative process often teaches us invaluable lessons. Watching users 'in the wild' as they use our products is the best way to find out what works, then we can act on that feedback. It's much better to learn these things early and be able to respond than to go too far down the wrong path." How might this idea of implementation, feedback, and iteration work in your school or classroom?

4. Look for ideas everywhere. Be inspired by different fields and different experts and different experiences. Read books on topics beyond your subject area—from authors outside education. Try to learn new things regularly—intellectually and physically. Talk to new people and bring your problems to different people, including experts in other fields. Truly embrace a diversity of perspectives and ideas.

I remember being a student teacher and being exposed to education theorist Jacob Kounin's idea of teacher *withitness*, the ability to seem "with it" by being aware of what's going on in the classroom. I can't help thinking that sort of mental acuity must be sharpened with practice—and is at least as meaningful in creating learning experiences as it is in maintaining classroom discipline. Neal Stephenson authored the popular science-fiction novel *Snow Crash*, which inspired much of our modern conception of virtual reality. He drew inspiration for his writing from fields as diverse as history, linguistics, anthropology, archaeology, religion, computer science, politics, cryptography, memetics, and philosophy. What is something you're always wanted to learn more about? Now is a good time to do a search, read some, and maybe even watch a YouTube video and try something yourself.

5. Share everything. "By sharing everything, you encourage the discussion, exchange and reinterpretation of ideas, which can lead to unexpected and innovative outcomes," notes Wojcicki. Having a strong professional learning network (PLN) and sharing ideas through social media and at online or in-person events gives you the power to multiply your knowledge, skills, and reach. In the Empowered Teachers chapter (up next!), you'll find a whole section devoted to the benefits of sharing with an online personal learning network. Is there something you've created recently in your role that might benefit others in similar roles if you shared it online?

6. Spark with imagination, fuel with data. Wild ideas can turn into awesome innovations. "What begins with intuition is fueled by insights. If you're lucky, these reinforce one another," writes Susan Wojcicki. You have to test intuitions and then adjust or pivot based on the results. By testing BreakoutEDU on real teachers, James Sanders found out what worked and what didn't and discovered ways to iterate and improve on his prototype. It's worth asking yourself how quickly you can test your idea. What is the "minimum viable" prototype you can get into people's hands to test right away?

7. Be a platform. The idea of being a platform plays off pillar five: Share everything. Google's open technologies make it easy for app developers to build on, add to, and expand the capabilities of its products. Again looking to Breakout EDU as an example, Sanders and his team didn't just create one game, they created a platform for other teachers to create their own games for all grade levels and all subject areas. At EdTechTeam, we didn't just create one presentation or professional development experience. We didn't just create one summit. We created a platform for thousands of teachers to share in their own regions around the world with a global audience. It can be transformational to ask yourself if your own best ideas might be more of a platform for others.

8. Never fail to fail. Rich DeVaul lists his title on LinkedIn as Director of Rapid Evaluation and Mad Science at Google [X]. I love that. He's a rapid prototyping specialist and was the chief technical architect for Project Loon. (He also keynoted one of the first EdTechTeam Summits in the Bay Area back in 2013.) He says his job is to fail fast. As the Project Loon story goes, DeVaul pitched an idea to Google's founders. They liked the idea, but instead of allowing him to run with it, they pointed out that the people who would benefit from it most weren't online yet. And they told him to fix that problem first.

CREATE A CULTURE OF SHARING AND INNOVATION

The best schools in the world are those where adults—especially teachers—feel comfortable sharing ideas, easily discussing things that don't go well, and creating resources to pass along to colleagues on and off their campuses. That's why, if I were dreaming up my ideal school, the ability to comfortably share ideas and resources would be a primary component. It may sound strange to those professionally outside education, but one of the biggest problems schools have is a reluctance to share stories of success effectively.

This reluctance may be based on the belief that openly discussing one teacher's successes represents a critique of other teachers' shortcomings. In this kind of setting, a leader who refers to a teacher's good work might be inadvertently creating the conditions for that teacher to be ostracized. This sort of dysfunctional atmosphere is distressingly common in schools. When considering how to overcome this poisonous lack of professional interaction, a good point of departure is understanding the substantial advantages of doing so, including the following:

Teachers can let go of the absurdity that we, as educators, never do anything wrong. The simple realization that every single one of us has room for improvement can allow for discussions that promote interesting and needed growth.

Students benefit from an environment in which we regularly ask one another for and act on ideas for varying our presentation and exploration of content to reach more of our classes.

When we don't come across as know-it-alls, conversations with parents and other stakeholders allow for new possibilities. Parents appreciate when we collaboratively discuss possibilities for fostering their children's new talents. You'll also find that community supporters may be more prepared to give their time and resources when we are open about how we are working to overcome the barriers we and our students face.

Perhaps most importantly, students tend to have a stronger rapport with teachers who talk *with* them rather than *at* them, and this better rapport can lead to more effective learning conditions. This includes getting students' feedback on how a class is going and how we can be better teachers for them, something I would do from time to time. When I'd have this conversation with my students, I would remind them that while I couldn't promise I would act on their suggestions, if they were willing to share their ideas (even the critical ones), I did feel I could improve.

We all fall into habits that work against our hopes for what we want to accomplish and how we want our students to respond. But maintaining open communication with our students and colleagues is a prerequisite for most, and perhaps all, substantive kinds of organizational improvement.

When we begin approaching how to build a better atmosphere to discuss possibilities for better teaching and learning, one of the first challenges we face is creating concrete avenues for identifying strengths. All too often, these strengths are hidden behind a silence—one brought on by an atmosphere that discourages discussing successes and can deprive both our students and teachers of moments they would treasure. With a clear sense of how to discuss and explore successes, however, a team can orient itself toward innovating in exciting ways.

Adapted from **Making Your School Something Special** *by Rushton Hurley*

DeVaul went to work on the problem of getting more people online around the globe and came up with the idea of offering 4G internet access through balloons in the stratosphere, where predictable wind patterns would allow them to navigate their location by adjusting their altitude. When DeVaul started working on the prototypes, his focus moved from ideation to failing fast. He created the first balloon as fast as he could, with the intention of getting it to wreck. Then he'd create another one, test it, and wreck it, all with the goal of creating a light but durable balloon that could handle changes in temperature and altitude. He and the Project Loon team spent months launching up to five prototypes a week to see what didn't work until they found an iteration that did.

The idea to apply when you're tackling a problem is to come up with a potential solution and try to break it. Test it. Look for the flaws. Try to fail fast—find out what doesn't work so that you can figure out what *does* work. For more ideas on this, keep reading. Failing is good for progress, and it requires risk.

Risk Taking

It doesn't take much to look at what Google is doing and make the connection between innovation and risk: If you're going to innovate, you're going to have to move beyond your comfort zone. You can't get to the Moon if you're not willing to build the spacecraft, climb inside, and "go for launch." And you can't do any of those things all by yourself; you need people with whom you can brainstorm and test ideas. You need feedback on what works—and what doesn't.

During the past two decades, a significant shift in the kinds of skills needed in the marketplace has taken place. In a collaborative report titled *enGauge 21st Century Skills: Literacy in the Digital Age*, researchers from North Central Regional Educational Laboratories (NCREL) and Metiri Group (way back in 2003) explained that "As technology becomes more prevalent in our everyday lives, cognitive skills become increasingly critical." Inventive thinking skills, which include adaptability, self-direction,

GUEST VOICE: CHRIS LEHMANN
DON'T JUST CHANGE, GET BETTER

Principal and CEO of Science Leadership Academy, @chrislehmann,

PracticalTheory.org, Philadelphia, Pennsylvania

Educational innovation has been plagued by the fact that education is a very reactionary sector. Anytime we try something new, it is inevitably imperfect. When anything goes wrong, people rush back to what they know, which is why you see textbooks on the desks and why the desks and rows persist even though no one thinks those setups are particularly good. They are what is known.

One of the times courageous leadership has to happen is when you have a vision of your school that is powerful and profound and maybe a little daring. You have to trust it, and you have to know that more often than not, the problems with your model are not necessarily best solved by changing the model, but by getting better at the model. **Developing that mindset of trial, error, and improvement is how we can avoid being reactionary.**

The courageous leader asks, "What is the worst consequence of our best idea?" You have to answer that question, and you have to own the fact that all ideas, even your best ones, are flawed. There is a dark side to even the best thing you do, and be prepared to go through an iterative process of wondering, questioning, problem-solving, and mitigating so you don't end up going down a reactionary path that moves you backward instead of forward. When things go wrong, have the courage to say, "We're going to stay the course. We must figure out how to do it better or get more people on board, or get the buy-in we need, or get stakeholders excited." Have the courage to iterate and improve; don't overcorrect or just blow in the wind.

A Message from the Future

Ask yourself: Are you creating the conditions such that the kids you serve feel like they can go out and change the world? Are you doing everything you can to create the conditions that empower kids to go out and be the citizens the world desperately needs them to be?

curiosity, creativity, risk taking, and sound reasoning (aka critical thinking), are all essential to our students' success in the marketplace as employees, innovators, and entrepreneurs. Because of that, they must be an intentional part of today's education. A focus on the Four Cs—critical thinking, communication, collaboration, and creativity—makes some of these essential skills priorities in many schools today.

Risk taking, however, is a skill that gets a lot more lip service than actual practice. The consequences for failing are simply too risky. Why would a teacher risk an innovative approach to learning when they can't be faulted for using the tried-and-true method and focusing on "the test" and, thus, job security? Why would students go off script regarding a project when the specified list provided in the rubric requires little creativity or effort? Failing comes at too great a cost in terms of points, grades, and GPA—none of which, incidentally, are terribly important to long-term success.

Risk Taking: The willingness to make mistakes, advocate for unconventional or unpopular positions, or tackle extremely challenging problems without obvious solutions, such that one's personal growth, integrity, or accomplishments are enhanced.

If we're going to teach risk taking, we have to make it okay to fail. That means it has to be okay for teachers to have a lesson completely fall flat or dissolve into chaos in front of the principal. If a principal looks at a teacher who has taken a risk—with inquiry-based learning projects or a new VR activity, for example—and says, "It was chaos in that room; you have to get control of your class," the teacher is not going to feel safe taking risks. But if, instead, the principal debriefs with the teacher after an observation or evaluation, applauds the risk, and encourages next steps, then suddenly it becomes a growth experience. Even if the lesson failed in the moment, the outcome is positive because it empowers the teacher to fail forward. What if a principal told all teachers at the school they had to crash five lessons this semester in order to speed up their improvements?

> ## If we're going to teach risk taking, we have to make it okay to fail.

The hesitancy to take risks isn't limited to students and teachers; principals, too, can be risk-avoiders—and often are. Just as it has to be okay for teachers to fail, superintendents and district leaders must allow principals to fail. School site leaders must have the freedom to develop new programs and try new technologies without feeling as if the district leadership is waiting to drop the ax. You can follow this all the way up the chain of command. The school board has to make it okay for district leadership to take risks and try new things. For that to happen, the community must allow for and encourage innovative programs (this ties into another area of the honeycomb, engaged community, which we'll get to in a later chapter). Risk requires courage for everyone involved. Anyone at any level of the system can take the first courageous steps, but if those first steps are taken by someone in a leadership role, the potential result is a bigger, more quickly felt impact.

Be Subversive

I want to wind up this chapter with some advice that has empowered me for a long time. Back in 2006, I was attending a panel session at NECC (National Educational Computing Conference, which later became the International Society for Education or ISTE Conference), and among the panelists was an educator from Australia named Tom March. He shared some of the great things that were happening in schools in Australia, everything from flexible learning spaces to Wikis, blogs, and podcasts—and I was impressed. At the same time, I knew that teachers in the States would hear those kinds of things and think, *My principal would never let me do that.* At the time, the United States was struggling with the "No

Child Left Behind" policy, and everybody was afraid to do anything that wasn't going to be on "the test."

So I asked, "What do you say to teachers who are in a school where the leadership doesn't support this kind of thing?"

Without skipping a beat, March said, "Be subversive." He went on to say that if you think you have a better way to teach or a better way to lead, try it out. And when you get great results (because you will), go share those results; show people how awesome whatever you're doing in the classroom is for students. So many of the schools we (EdTechTeam) have visited work from the perspective that the path to doing amazing things is to go for it, to do it (whatever it is that creates the best opportunities for learning) anyway. Think about your goal as an educator. Is it scores on a test? Or is it developing compassionate and passionate global citizens who work with others to solve meaningful problems? From my perspective, the goal of education is to equip the thinkers of tomorrow who can push the boundaries of society, science, and industry. Yes, that can happen if you teach to the test and the standards when you include project-based learning and inquiry of some kind. But the bigger risk, and I think a bigger payoff, is to say, "Forget the test; we, as a community, are committing to (fill in the blank with your vision)."

> ## If you think you have a better way to teach or a better way to lead, try it.

The reality is teachers often work from the perspective that they "have to" teach a certain way. There's this vicious cycle where the teacher says, "Oh, no, no, no. I can't do all that new-fangled stuff because of the test. My principal would fire me for sure."

The principal says, "I know the test is not really important for our students' personal and future success, but the district says we've got to focus on scores."

GUEST VOICE: MICHAEL LUBELFELD
PARTNER WITH YOUR COMMUNITY

Superintendent, North Shore School District 112, Highland Park, Illinois,

Former Superintendent (2013–2018), Deerfield, Illinois,

@mikelubelfeld, dps109supt.edublogs.org, Deerfield, Illinois

In our community, we have made successful changes by reaching out to and engaging with our parent population and members of the business community in meaningful partnerships. An example of that partnership for us was coming together as a community of leaders, parents, administrators, students, teachers, and members of the board to redo twelve science labs that were around sixty years old. The cost was $8 million, and it was all done in an integrated approach through listening, leading, and learning. I'm really proud of that collaboration.

We had to be courageous enough to admit we had a problem: Our facilities were no longer relevant and we were not able to meet the needs of the present, let alone the future. We listened to our students, teachers, and experts; and we created spaces, learning, and curriculum that are inventive, innovative, and collaboratively designed. We extended a hand to the people in our community and asked them to join us on the journey. In the end, we funded the project with the support of our public.

Listen to your teachers and students so you can understand their needs. Then connect and collaborate with experts who can help your staff and students succeed. Communicate with your community leaders, business people in your area, and with parents. Be the one who connects the elements that help get learning off the ground.

A Message from the Future

Know your core values. Remember that you're a leader: You're not there to make everyone happy. In this business, the core value is making sure to support the social, emotional, and academic development and growth of children and the teachers who serve them. Be courageous, kind, and honest, and stay true to your core values.

On up the chain of command, the district leaders and superintendent say, "Oh, I'd much rather see kids creating and doing projects, but the board wants me to blah, blah, blah."

If you talk to the school board, you'll hear, "Well, we're really only requiring this because it's what the voters expect. The test scores are in the newspaper, and they want to see test scores go up."

Then you go talk to parents and they say, "I don't care about test scores; we're only doing all this crazy homework because the teacher told us to."

Then you're right back at the beginning of the circle, with the teacher teaching to the test. I've never talked to anybody who is actually involved with education that cares about test scores. Nobody. They all point to somebody else in some larger context beyond their control. I remember working with a public school board officer named Dana Black in the Newport-Mesa Unified School District here in California, who understood this need for *someone* to step out and take that risk to break the cycle. She inspired everyone in the room when she reminded us that education agencies are really under no compulsion to get great test scores. She said, "If we as a community decide that our own goals are more important to us than test scores, then we can announce that, and we can move toward those goals."

The district and school leaders who realize they actually *already have the autonomy* to drive the vision for learning—meaning they don't need to ask for permission to launch initiatives that empower teachers, or allow for student agency, or provide the tools and infrastructure to support that vision—are the ones who get the extraordinary results that everyone

> **Although anyone at any point in the cycle can break it, teachers, principals, or community members, it's even better if it starts with top levels of leadership.**

points to and wants to emulate. What's interesting is that the school leaders and teachers at those forward-thinking, innovative schools don't necessarily see themselves as anything other than a school that started with the same challenging context as everyone else. But they were willing to step out and break the cycle based on their convictions. Although anyone at any point in the cycle can break it, teachers, principals, or community members, it's even better if it starts with top levels of leadership. As Mike Lubelfeld, a superintendent in Deerfield, Illinois notes, "It takes a great deal of courage to lead with your core values even when people around you may not understand that the right thing to do today is different from what it was yesterday. There's going to be vocal opposition, and it's going to be politically challenging, even when the opportunity will yield strong instructional benefits." Do it anyway.

School change requires courageous leadership. It isn't always easy, and sometimes you have to work around the system to improve it, but the results are worth it.

Guest Voice: Nick Polyak
Listen, Serve, Support

Superintendent, Leyden High School District 212, @npolyak, #suptchat, Franklin Park, Illinois

Our schools don't exist in a vacuum. Every community has its unique needs, and the schools need to be responsive and reinvent themselves continually to be relevant wherever they are. We should be preparing kids with the skills necessary to fuel jobs in their own communities and to be competitive on a global scale. When I think of courageous leadership, I think of humility and approaching leadership positions—be it a district or building level—from a service mindset. Leadership is not about keeping score of who accomplishes what; it's about what the kids are getting and what's happening in our schools.

In our district, we're trying to give voice to our students. We're also trying to give voice to our staff in terms of how we operate. A couple years ago, we created a teacher group called the Innovation Incubators. We released the teachers from their departmental professional learning communities (PLCs) and said, "Your task is to think big and bring ideas back to us. You can scale up something we're already doing, or you can experiment with a completely new idea." The group developed a school-within-a-school model for incoming freshman called Co.Lab. The idea was to create a fully project-based, interdisciplinary track for incoming freshmen. That program is going to launch next year, and it was completely developed by a group of our teachers to whom we gave the freedom to think differently.

It takes courage to let go and trust those around you and then to implement their ideas—to create a culture where it's okay to think differently.

The courageous effort for leaders when it comes to listening to student and teacher voices is to say, "Alright, I support what you came up with," instead of saying, "I want you to do XYZ." It takes courage to let go and trust those around you and then to implement their ideas—to create a culture where it's okay to think differently. Your people have to know that you're going to help them—not fire them—if something goes sideways. Things will go wrong. Expect that. In a culture of innovation, that's okay. But when you really listen to those you serve and then support them in their efforts to take school to the next level, you'll discover that it's easy to start a new program when it has a grassroots origin.

A Message from the Future

Embrace flexibility as an individual and as an organization because what made people successful in the past is different from what makes them successful today. What kids are going to need in the future will be different still. As a leader, you need to be nimble, flexible, and agile so you can constantly reinvent education to make it what kids in your schools need right now.

CHAPTER THREE
EMPOWERED TEACHERS

A good teacher isn't someone who gives the answers but is understanding of needs and challenges— and gives tools to help other people succeed.
–Justin Trudeau, Canadian Prime Minister

> **Empowered teachers are passionate educators with the tools, professional development, and time to create engaging experiences for students.**

Empowered teachers often look and act a lot like courageous leaders. They are passionate educators who offer a vision to their students. They seek out opportunities for growth. They are connected educators who develop their own personal learning networks. And they are essential for driving school change. A school can have an amazing, courageous leader, but without teachers who are empowered and equipped, change either doesn't happen or it doesn't last when the leader moves on.

Courageous leaders know that to empower their teachers, they need to provide the tools, training, and time for teachers to learn, plan, connect, and collaborate. Empowered teachers know that to create the best learning experiences for their students, they need to be proactive and intentional about using tools, seeking out professional development, and maximizing their time. Let's discuss the tools first.

Equip to Empower

Empowered teachers are passionate about finding and incorporating the best practices into their classrooms to ensure students are empowered themselves. The tools they use equip them to create engaging learning experiences—experiences that give students ownership over learning and allow teachers to assess what students actually understand and are capable of. At EdTechTeam events, attendees always want to know, "What's the best app for teaching math?" or "What's the best computer for one-to-one classrooms?" or "What's the best program for formative assessment?" There are great tools out there for all those things, and we certainly share about them at our events, but rather than focusing in on a very specific app for science or math, or software that does one specific thing, I like to point people toward open-ended tools.

I believe the most valuable tools are those that allow teachers to create great experiences for kids—regardless of the subject matter. To me, that's where tools like Google Docs or Minecraft or audio and video editing tools come into play. Tools that have the greatest potential to change the culture of a school bring elements of creation and collaboration. The most important tools are those that change the teachers' relationships with their students and change the students' relationships with their peers. The truth is any specific tool matters less than the way you use it. Heather Dowd, coauthor of *Classroom Management in the Digital Age,* explains it this way: "It's not about one tool; it's about the big picture. What do you want students to do? Once you know the capabilities of a tool and understand what's possible, you can start thinking bigger. You can stop looking at an app or a device as 'a tool for English,' for example, and start thinking about it in terms of what those things give us access to that we didn't have before."

So, for example, you can choose to look at the camera on a phone or tablet as a distraction or as a tool. Heather says she believes that cameras on students' tech devices are among the most underutilized and important tools, and they're everywhere. "You can use a camera to record thinking and record writing—for any subject," she says. "I taught physics and math, so I always get pushback from the physics and the math teachers who say tech devices aren't really for them. And sure, you don't want to solve physics problems by typing them on a device, but you can use the camera to record your thinking on a physics problem. Or you can give your students a problem with the wrong answer or something wrong in it and then they have to record themselves talking through the problems and finding the error. The camera is simply one way to make thinking visible."

The Gift of Time

I mentioned in the previous chapter that risk taking is part of great, courageous leadership. That's true for district and building leaders *and* for teachers who lead the way in their classrooms, departments, and schools. And there's no question that using new technology (or using technology in new ways) feels like a risk. When we talk about using new tools—whether specific apps or looking at tech in broad strokes—we have to discuss how those tools get introduced and integrated into a school's culture. Very often, the introduction happens through professional development. It may be required sessions offered by a district or school, or it may be training that teachers seek out on their own through books, podcasts, blogs, and conferences. Regardless, good training is integral to the success of empowered teachers.

Professional Development from the Courageous Leader's Perspective

While I was working as a high school technology coordinator, I was introduced to a simple and practical guideline for funding educational technology initiatives: If a school or district received funding to spend on edtech, only one third of that money should be spent on stuff—computers, devices, software, etc. One third should be saved for technical support, and one third of the funds should go toward PD to support teachers as they learn to use the new technology. Through the years, as the need for

Guest Voice: Heather Dowd
Make the Shift, Think Bigger

Learning Designer and Coach, Dynamic Learning Project Mentor,

@heza, hdowd.com, Illinois

It used to be that the teacher was the person with all the knowledge. If we think back to the beginning of schools, the only place where people could get that kind of knowledge was from teachers and books. And now, it's completely shifted. There's more knowledge available on the internet than any one person could ever possess, and all of it can be *googled*. Technology and access to information changes our role as teachers—a truth some teachers embrace more easily than others. Some people are comfortable with the fact that students can look up anything online, and they understand that we have to ask students non-*googleable* questions. I think there are still a number of people uncomfortable with that.

One way to get comfortable with this shift in education is to partner with other teachers who are already making these changes, using technology in the classroom, and finding meaningful ways to assess learning. Sometimes, all it takes is for people to see what's possible—to see someone who has overcome a challenge. When you can see that, it's easier to say, "Oh, yeah, I can do that." But if there's nobody in your district or in your school who is doing things differently, change feels more difficult, and it feels unreachable. So just get out there, go to different events, and network with people. Once you see what's possible, you can start thinking even bigger.

A Message from the Future

Your biggest fears concerning technology will (most likely) not come to fruition. Will there be broken screens and lost laptops? Probably. Things won't go perfectly, and you'll need a plan B. But most of the fears that teachers, parents, and administrators have about handing technology over to kids don't happen. I think that's true for many of the fears we have with the changes that we want to make in school.

tech support has leveled off a bit, the percentages might be slightly different, but the principle still applies. If you have $100,000 to spend, don't go out and buy ten class sets of Chromebooks. Instead, buy three (or four) sets. Then, make sure you have the tech support you need to keep them running properly and provide training to your teachers so they learn how maximize the use of those tools in their classrooms. (See the sidebar, "5 Philosophies for Effective Professional Development" for ideas on what to look for when booking your next speaker or selecting a conference.)

Right alongside the need for training is the need for teachers to have time and space to explore, play with, and learn to use new tools. School leaders must build time into the formal schedule of the school day for teachers to collaborate and to try new things. Offering teachers the gift of time to play, explore, and get comfortable with tools is critical. Different schools find different solutions for this, but a typical solution is to say, "You have Wednesday afternoon off to collaborate with your team or PLC (professional learning community)." If your school has started using G Suite, teachers can use that PLC time to learn how to make the best use of that system. Or maybe they use a prep period once a week to simply play with Google's apps or Flipgrid or whatever other tech tool your school is using. The point is, teachers need time that can be devoted to trying things out and working with other teachers to share best practices. Don't fill all your professional development hours with training; allot some of that precious time—on a regular basis—for teachers to get to know the tools. Call it a gift—the gift of time.

Professional Development from the Empowered Educator's Perspective

Ideally, you work in a district or school that devotes ample resources and time to professional development. Whether that's true or not, I have a question for you: Who do you learn from on a regular basis? When I ask this question at our EdTechTeam events, the responses vary. Some say, "The other teachers in my grade level (or department)," or, "The other

5 Philosophies for Effective Professional Development

The Lead Learner Philosophy—Early on in my career in edtech consulting and training, I heard former CUE CEO Mike Lawrence share a Native American proverb that has stuck with me: "He who learns from one who is learning drinks from a flowing river." I suppose you can take that metaphor a bit further and add that the last thing you want to do is drink from stagnant water—or learn from people who aren't learning themselves. My philosophy is that it is always a leader's responsibility to be the lead learner. Whenever and wherever people are learning and are committed to sharing their learning, the ideas and innovation grow. As courageous leaders and empowered teachers propel professional development opportunities, whether they are bringing in experts, attending off-site workshops, or offering the training themselves, the best learning always occurs when the trainer is the lead learner—someone who knows he or she always has something to learn from others.

The Face-to-Face Philosophy—Information transmission cannot replace face-to-face learning—whether it's in the classroom or a professional development setting. Podcasts, video, social media chats, and webcasts are great; I encourage people to use them. But there is something to be said for the opportunity to tap into the talent, creative energy, and expertise of the people who are in the room with you. For the educator, there is no replacement for being able to see in someone's eyes when they are frustrated or excited—and being able to look over their shoulder and see why. Connecting and collaborating with people in real life is a powerful way to enhance the learning experience.

The Kindergarten Philosophy—My wife is a kindergarten teacher, and her philosophy on learning is that every positive learning experience is a one-dollar deposit in a her students' "love-of-learning bank." Every negative experience they have is a ten-dollar withdrawal. This is as true in her class of five-year-olds as it is with a room of adults at a technology conference. When people get frustrated and quit using technology because they can't figure it out, schools lose. Great training acknowledges the ten-to-one ratio and ensures that although people may feel challenged, they come away with a positive learning experience.

The "And Life" Philosophy—Pets and babies teach people more about technology than training sessions ever will. By that I mean true learning happens when the content is relevant or meaningful to teachers in some way. Don't be afraid to allow people to tap into their passions, interests, and personal lives as they learn and explore technology tools. Seeing and sharing cute pictures of pets and babies (or grandbabies) motivates people to learn and try and do. Ultimately, as they explore, they become comfortable using the technology and find the courage to use it in the classroom with their students.

The Race Car Philosophy—Before my boys were born, I dreamed of pursuing race car driving as a hobby once I finished my dissertation. Then our two boys, Clark and Finn, came along, and of course, my plans and hobbies changed. But I still remember what I learned regarding focus from a book called *Speed Secrets* by race car driver Ross Bentley. He said that when you're driving a race car, you don't just focus on where you are—that would be foolish in any vehicle no matter how fast it's going. Neither do you focus only on the immediate next turn. Instead, you look as far down the road as you can because the way you make a turn affects the way you come out of it, which affects the way you enter the straightaway, which affects your overall lap time. Race car drivers will walk a track and plan the lines they'll drive before even getting in their cars. Then they'll drive the track slowly. In education, we don't have that luxury, but we can still look several turns down the road to where we'd like our practice to be in the future. My challenge to you, as you're learning new things or introducing new technology to your staff, is this: don't just think about the skill or tool you're learning about or training on today. Consider how the tool or practice can help you get where you want to be one year, three years, five years down the road. Start now to plan and move and grow in that direction because that's how you'll help students create the future they deserve.

principals in my district." Or I might hear from a librarian who says, "I collaborate with the librarians at the other two high schools." Some might say, "I'm on this great listserv," and, of course, at every session I eventually hear someone say, "I learn from my students." Our EdTechTeam Summits and workshops as well as ISTE conferences and EdCamps are mentioned. But aside from some of those larger conferences, surprisingly few people mention learning from people outside their local area. Even today, few educators mention Twitter and online connections as the source of regular learning opportunities. When I was a new teacher, that was my experience, too. Teaching was pretty isolating, and it wasn't all that easy to find the help I needed. I remember going to an assistant principal once for help with a kid, and he literally said, "That's your job," and stormed off. In retrospect, I see how lucky I was to be in an English department that had an "English lounge," where others in the department would hang out during breaks or at lunch. Occasionally, a social studies teacher would join us, but on most days, there were six to eight other professionals whom I could ask for help—or commiserate with. Three or four of them taught in my grade level, which meant I had access to a shared file cabinet where I could pull out old lesson plans and create new things with them. Over time, I've realized even that level of collaboration was unusual.

If you're a teacher, you know what I mean when I say you are *lucky* if you have someone on your campus with whom you can collaborate. But if you're the one art teacher or the assistant principal in charge of discipline, you aren't that lucky. And if you are in education technology or are a progressive integrator of technology, you may feel like the lone nut on campus. But it doesn't have to be that way. There's a whole world of connections waiting to help you online.

I really got plugged into my online PLN in 2004, first with blogs and a few years later with Twitter. I had just started my doctorate work in 2003, and unequivocally, during the next five years, my PLN taught me more and had a bigger impact on my career than my doctoral program, although that was a fantastic learning and growing experience too. Today, in addition to a wealth of blogs and Twitter chats, there are podcasts,

Facebook groups, Google communities, and countless other opportunities to connect with other like-minded people online. Many of my friends and colleagues also share their Oculus Go accounts in a Facebook group so we can connect in virtual reality too! You may be an auditory learner who prefers listening to content, or maybe you're like me and you really like to read and write. The choice is yours, and you don't have to choose just one medium or one platform. Whatever your preferred learning style or area of focus, there are hundreds, *thousands*, of people ready to connect with you, teach you, and learn from you.

Sarah Thomas, CEO and founder of EduMatch.org, says all those opportunities to connect and learn and grow are what make this an exciting time to be an educator. "We have the option to take our professional development and careers into our own hands. It's the democratization of education in a way. In the past, you had a few select people telling you what you needed to know. Now, with social media and just by changing our mindsets, we're seeing that more people are taking the power back to find what they want to learn, to find what they're passionate about, and how they can use that to benefit students."

That's empowerment and, as Sarah Thomas says, "It really brings back the art to teaching. The major game changer for me happened when I started choosing what I wanted to learn rather than just waiting to receive top-down type learning."

The ability to take control of your PD by connecting with other educators today is phenomenal. However you choose to connect and whatever you want to learn, the experience of learning from and with people all over the world—people who have different perspectives, different experiences, and different resources—eclipses what any one school or a few professors can offer.

Make the Most of Your PLN

Connect—Whichever tool you're using to grow your PLN, the goal is to make connections. So if you're reading and writing blogs, be sure to reply in the comments. If you're on Twitter, be sure to reply to posts, like them, and re-tweet them. If you're using podcasts, post a response on the pod-cast page. If you're watching a video by an educator on YouTube, leave a comment. If you're on Facebook, like the post, share it, or leave a reply. Connect with those people in some way. Don't just be a lurker.

Contribute—As you develop your PLN, think of it as a community. You build social capital in the community by contributing in some way. When I first started blogging, I was working full-time in addition to doing my coursework for my PhD. At first, although I knew I wanted to contribute to the community that I was learning from, I thought, *There's no way I have time to add blogging to my schedule*. But what I realized was that any of the writing I was doing for school or for work was content I could share on my blog. From then on, whenever what I was writing might be relevant to somebody else, I shared it online. And that turned out to be really pow-erful in terms of discussing ideas and learning *with* others.

If you've created a great internet-safety lesson for third graders, post that, because other third-grade teachers may find that useful. Even if you have tough questions and no answers, post those because you'll learn something from the people who respond, and the discussion might be useful to other people as well.

Converse—As you contribute consistently through blogs, Twitter, Facebook posts, podcasts, or however you like to share, people will leave comments or ask questions, and the opportunity to connect continues. When I started blogging, I was writing about the things I was researching and learning in my PhD work. As I shared things online that I had written for school, the researchers I had cited would comment on my blog. I also connected with teachers who were actually doing the things I had been researching in their classrooms. They shared their stories of those real-life experiences in the comments of my blog—and in some cases pointed me toward their blogs. The point is, by making contributions to my PLN by blogging, I received much in return in terms of building new relationships and learning through the conversations that developed, even when they weren't necessarily focused on education.

GUEST VOICE: SARAH THOMAS, PhD
MAKE TIME TO CONNECT

Regional Tech Coordinator, Founder and CEO of EduMatch.org,

@sarahdateechur, sarahjanethomas.com,

Washington, DC area

When people say, "I don't have time for social media," I always think, *People make time for what they believe is important.* If people see the potential value in something, they give it a shot, and then they'll probably find the value they were hoping for. And if not, then at least they tried.

So if you don't have much time (And who does?), my advice is to give building your PLN online as much time as you can give. It doesn't have to be your whole life. If you have five minutes a day or five minutes a week, that's enough to check your Twitter notifications, make a friend, check in with someone from your PLN, or just be an accountability buddy. From there, scaffold it. Just see how much time you have to give. Many times, you'll find social media can be a time *saver* because you can ask questions, collaborate with others, and spend less time searching for answers.

When the opportunities present themselves to connect and learn and try something new, jump in feet first. Don't go crazy and jump in headfirst, but definitely be willing to take risks. **Even small risks have the potential to make a big change,** so do it; don't let that moment pass by.

A Message from the Future

We need more people to share their stories, because the more perspective we get on ideas, the more likely we are to find the solution that fits our situation. What might be right for one classroom or one student is not necessarily right for all, so the more that people share what works, the more we can find solutions for each student.

Request—Developing relationships and making contributions means that when the time comes that you need help, your request might fall on fertile soil. I love to show this how this works in real time when I'm doing a workshop. Early in the day, I'll post a question for my PLN, something like, "I'm with teachers in Minnesota. Why should they care about curating their own online personal learning network?" Within the hour and throughout the next day, I'll be able to share many responses, no matter the day of the week, time of day, or time zone I post in.

What Are You Going to Do to Build Your PLN?

Wondering where to start? Here are a few ideas:

- **Live Events**—Nothing beats the energy of live events. Whether it's one of EdTechTeam's summits or workshops, an EdCamp in a nearby community, or a local meet-up with teachers in your district, there is power in connecting with people face to face.

- **Blogging**—Share your stories and experiences on a blog. There are a number of free blog platforms that are easy to get started on. Blogging empowers you to use your voice and contribute to important conversations in a meaningful way.

- **Twitter**—Turns out you can say a lot in 280 characters or fewer. Twitter has one of the most active platforms for educators. Search for a hashtag like #morenow, #edtechteam, #edchat, #edumatch, or #suptchat to connect with people on specific topics. Weekly Twitter chats are fast-paced and fun ways to join the conversation and meet new people. Check out the #PubPD hashtag for a clever approach to online professional development while meeting face-to-face with other teachers for drinks!

- **Facebook**—Facebook groups can be a great place to connect with people from around the world who share a common interest or teach in the same subject area or grade level. Join us in the EdTechTeam group, the Facebook Education group, or do a search for any topic to find your tribe. Facebook also offers a platform for hosting live video with real-time interaction for a global audience.

- **Google+ Groups**—On Google Plus, you can find many groups related to all facets of education. Join us at the EdTechTeam Global Community or search for a topic you care about, and join the conversation!

- **Pinterest**—Need an idea for a bulletin board, an #inquiryproject, or classroom management strategy? Check out Pinterest. Have a great idea to share? Pin it!

- **Instagram**—This is the place to share learning with a focus on the visual and an emphasis on quick stories. Share pictures and videos of learning in action, or better yet, let kids do the sharing.

- **Snapchat**—Extremely popular with younger teachers (and older students), Snapchat can be used for fast, targeted messages—without the pressure of a permanent feed. Student use can include "BookSnaps" or short snapshots of learning.

- **Voxer**—Many school leaders and teachers use Voxer as a communication tool in their school communities, but it's also a way to connect with educators around the world. EduMatch.org uses Voxer to host its annual EdCamp Voice, where people meet online to talk and learn about education. Naturally, it's a great option for auditory learners (as are podcasts, which tend to be more like a show than a conversation).

- **YouTube**—Want to do, well, anything? There's probably a how-to video on YouTube. After Google, this is the world's most popular search engine, and it's a great place to learn and share your learning via video. It's also the perfect platform for giving students the experience of sharing their work with an authentic audience.

- **Chat Services**—Sometimes direct messages or group chats are more appropriate than more public social media. EdTechTeam hosts chats in Google Hangouts for various programs. Internally, we use Slack, a real-time threaded message application, for communication. Many organizations are experimenting with Slack as a community online learning platform. Geography factors into the choice of chat service; for example, WhatsApp is very popular outside the United States for texting via internet. And of course, if you want to move from text to video you can jump into a Hangout, FaceTime, or Skype call in the moment.

You can find me, @MarkWagner, on Twitter (connect with me on other social media channels by visiting MoreNowBook.com). You can also connect with EdTechTeam's resources and community using @EdTechTeam.

The Strength of Weak Ties

David Jakes, an educational technologist and design consultant you'll hear more from later in this book, used to write a blog titled *The Strength of Weak Ties*. Over time, the title became more and more meaningful to me, and I often referenced it in my workshops. Eventually, I asked Jakes how he chose his blog's title. The next day, he posted a response on his blog, addressed to my workshop attendees, and he explained that the title came from Malcolm Gladwell's book *The Tipping Point*. Gladwell argues that it's not the people we're closest to that we learn the most from. It's often the people with whom we have weak connections who teach us the most.

The strength of weak ties comes, in part, from the fact that if you throw a broad net and reach out to people with whom you're not closely connected—people outside your school, district, or community networks—you're more likely to get information and perspectives that challenge you. Our close friends and coworkers tend to have a similar worldview, similar experiences, and similar resources at hand. If, however, we jump on Twitter or participate in an online class, or read a blog by someone in another state or country, we can connect with people who have

GUEST VOICE: WENDY GORTON
FIND (AND GIVE) HELP WHEN NEEDED

Executive Director of Global Community, EdTechTeam, @WendyGorton,

Portland, Oregon

When teachers need support, they need it right then. Forums like Google+ and Facebook groups provide a place for almost-instant interaction. When you're in a school, you can ask one person, but when you're online, you can interact with different people with different perspectives from all over.

One of the most powerful things we can do as teachers is to share with our community. Don't just be a lurker. Engage. Ask questions and respond to others' questions. Eventually, you'll get comfortable enough to go out there and share what you're doing as a teacher in your classroom. That's when people will start seeing you as a leader.

A Message from the Future

Keep connecting, and be brave enough to become a producer of information to share your voice not only with your smaller groups but with global audiences. Also, make sure to keep connecting with people in person and connecting with nature. Maintain a balance of growing digital connections, but also stay grounded by making time for the physical as well.

different experiences, perspectives, and resources—and we're more likely to learn something new from them. As an example, when I started doing online courses for my doctoral work, I took a class with a woman who was a tech coordinator in Iran. Another woman in the class was an African-American single mom from the south. Both of these educators had much different perspectives and life experiences than I did. Learning what they were doing in their schools and in their communities helped me take off my cultural blinders and see how others handle education.

Those kinds of experiences and relationships are common for me now, but I remember them and the impact they had on the way I thought regarding education because, at the time, connecting with people so far outside my own local bubble was completely foreign and new. I truly value having a diverse PLN. It means I'm never the only expert in the room. When I'm presenting to other educators or preparing a lesson for students, I can draw on the expertise of people all over the globe. The same can be true for you.

There is power in weak ties—in learning from people who have different backgrounds, experiences, and perspectives. You don't need to know everybody you connect with on Twitter or Facebook, and even if you've been connected a long time, you don't need to know them well personally. But it is good to take advantage of the strength of those weak ties because those are the people whose perspectives can teach you the most.

One more thing to remember: If you're new to Twitter or other social media platforms, the massive amount of information available can seem overwhelming. But just as you don't need to know everyone you connect with online, you also don't have to read everything that everyone posts. That would be impossible! Think of social media like a river. You know the river's always there for you to take a swim. You don't have to worry about seeing all of the river as it goes by. You can just stick your toes in or wade around in it for a little bit if you want; and it's there if you really want to go for a swim. But you can also get out and take a break for a while. If you're worried you're going to miss something important, you can always do a hashtag search to catch up on your favorite topic.

Empowered Teachers Empower Students

Empowered teachers are connected, and those connections create a diffusion of innovation as peers collaborate worldwide, share ideas, and inspire one another. Empowered teachers are also equipped and educated; they have access to systems, tools, and support that enable them to create engaging learning opportunities for their students. And empowered teachers empower students by giving them guidance and agency as well as access to tools and the freedom to create and collaborate with others. Student agency is where we're headed next on our tour of the honeycomb, and it's where students (and everyone else) discover the potential they have to make the world a better place—starting now.

CHAPTER FOUR
STUDENT AGENCY

Steve Jobs' focus on the user experience above all else has always been an inspiration to me.

—Larry Page, CEO and cofounder of Google

> ## Student agency is a focus on helping students find, organize, and use information to create, collaborate, and share in ways that are meaningful to them and to others in the outside world.

"What would school look like if you designed it from scratch today?" I was driving back from an event in Los Angeles with Steven Glyer, who was the educational technology director at Newport-Mesa Unified School District and my boss at the time, when he posed the question. I remember not having a good answer at the time. Several years later, I realized that the answer was that school should look a lot more like the offices at Google or Facebook than traditional school buildings.

On a Google Campus, you see stand-up desks, exercise balls as chairs, nap pods, microkitchens for snacks, and yes, even massage rooms. Work spaces are shared and collaborative, and there are quiet rooms for calls or concentration. In short, it's a place where it's good to be human.

Schools today can look like this; in fact, some already do (consider Albany Senior High School, for instance). But inspiring spaces (which we'll get into more in the next chapter) are only one factor in the equation for creating innovative, forward-thinking schools where students thrive. Culture plays an equally important role.

As my thoughts about what school could be—*should* be—continued to take shape over the next few years, they ended up looking a lot like the honeycomb of school change. Schools need courageous leaders and empowered teachers. And, most importantly, the schools of the future will be filled with students whose learning focuses not on memorizing facts and figures but on *how to learn* and *how to work together*. In these schools, students and teachers will have access to the technology, resources, and spaces that make learning engaging, interesting, and even fun. These schools will be places where students can *create, collaborate, and share in ways that are meaningful to them—and to others in the outside world.*

Sounds good, doesn't it? Here's the good news: We can take the first step into the future right now by asking students one simple question.

What Do You Want to Learn?

This question, *What do you want to learn?* is an effective way to start students down a pathway for meaningful learning. Every student has an answer. And when we ask students what *they* want to learn, we engage one of the keys to student motivation: Learning is fun, or at least interesting, if the topic is something they care about.

The reality is that we can't possibly prepare kids for their future; they're going to be working in jobs that don't exist yet and using technology we can't even imagine. Our job is no longer to help kids memorize a few things they might need some day; our job is to help kids access and use information in meaningful ways when they need it. Our job is to teach kids how to learn. And there's no better way to light that fire than to invite students to learn about things they care about. That's why, over and over again, I come back to questions like, "What do you want to learn?" and "What do you want to change about the world?"

When we ask kids what they want to learn or what they care about, and then help them achieve those goals, they can apply those learning techniques to whatever they do in the future. That's what student agency is all about. All over the world, innovative schools are setting the example for student-designed and student-led learning, and the outcomes are changing kids' lives by getting them excited about learning and, in some cases, the things they learn are changing the world.

> **Our job is no longer to help kids memorize a few things they might need some day; our job is to help kids access and use information in meaningful ways when they need it.**

When I was a high school English teacher, my students had a year-long senior project. They selected and researched a topic and had to work a certain number of hours in an internship in their chosen industry. They also had to create something, and then present their work to a panel of teachers and community members.

For the most part, students could choose to learn whatever they wanted. Some of their choices were surprising; for example, a varsity football player, whom no one would have expected to excel in English, or on a year-long project for that matter, decided to be trained as a chef for his senior project. He did all kinds of research on what it means to be a chef and what kind of education he would need. He took cooking classes and interned at a restaurant. He then built his own demo kitchen, complete with wheels so he could roll it into the school for his presentation, and a mirrored panel on top so those of us watching his presentation could see what he was doing. I was blown away, and the food was really good!

Another student came to me at the beginning of the year and said, "Hey, Wagner, I want to do Impalas." He was referring, of course, to the classic Chevy—his favorite car.

"Okay, man, we're doing Impalas for your senior project," I said, still not entirely sure where a project on Impalas was going to go.

By the end of the year, he had learned how to use AutoCAD® to design custom body parts for the cars and learned a few mechanical skills while interning in a body shop. Through the experience in the shop, he also learned what it took to run a small business. The project served as a huge gateway into all sorts of learning, all because he thought Impalas were cool.

Over and over again, I've seen how student agency and student-directed learning has that kind of gateway effect on learning, whether they are seniors in high school or kindergartners. My wife, Eva, used to have a segment in her kindergarten class that was aptly called "Ask Google" time. Students would use her phone to ask Google whatever they wanted to know. It was an exercise in diction for the kindergartners. They had to speak clearly enough that Google could understand them. They also had to learn to ask questions that made sense, even if they were about unicorns or kittens or Iron Man. And of course, the more questions they asked, the more questions they had. So something as simple as finding out what a child wanted to Ask Google proved to be a gateway into learning. (By the way, asking kids to write about their favorite video games can motivate reluctant writers whether they're in kindergarten or twelfth grade!)

A Transfer of Power

When we ask students what they want to learn, it's then essential that we empower them with the tools and time (sound familiar?) to explore their interests in ways that lead to meaningful learning. An element of Google's culture that fits extremely well in this idea of student agency is 20 percent time. At Google, employees are expected to use 80 percent of their time doing what they were hired to do—report to their managers, work on their projects, and hit their OKRs (objectives and key results). They are encouraged to dedicate 20 percent of their time to working on projects of their own devising—something they are passionate about. This 20 percent time has actually been an innovation engine at Google, allowing people to launch new products, work in small teams, and to innovate without bureaucracy weighing them down.

One of the tools that came out of a 20 percent time project is Gmail. The email product was started by a Googler who was frustrated by how poorly his email client handled the volume of email he received. During his 20 percent time, he started writing a new, web-based email program. Today, Gmail is the cornerstone of G Suite and everything the company does for business and education. Google Scholar, Google News, and even the ability to tap to call a business number returned in a mobile Google search are all examples of products that came out of 20 percent time projects.

Perhaps you've heard of teachers who are using 20 percent time, Genius Hour, or inquiry-based learning in their classrooms. And you may be wondering why it's such a big deal. You aren't alone if you think these projects seem like one more thing to add to an already-packed schedule. Or maybe you really are interested in incorporating this kind of student-driven learning into your school or classroom but wonder, *What do I do if kids want to learn about something that doesn't fit in the curriculum?* (Go back and read the story of the senior project on Impalas. *Any* student-directed project can lead to meaningful learning if you are purposeful and intentional about providing guidance as the adult and educator in the room. Students can meet language-arts standards writing about any topic, and as math teachers know, math is in everything, even, if not especially, fast cars.)

Increasing student agency by asking students what they want to learn isn't about free-for-all learning.

Increasing student agency by asking students what they want to learn isn't about free-for-all learning (although I'm not sure that would be a bad idea). It's about changing the mindsets surrounding education. It's about transferring power from the teacher to the student—or rather, accepting the reality that the power shift is already happening in our world where information can be accessed 24/7. It's about preparing our students for the future by teaching them how to learn and showing them what they are capable of accomplishing.

Kevin Brookhouser, author of *The 20time Project*, says that getting students to recognize that they have the ability to make a real difference in the world is crucial in the transition to student agency. "One of my main missions is to get students to think of themselves as people who can solve big problems," Kevin Brookhouser explains. "The world we're handing off to these students is one that has some really significant problems that we adults have not yet been able to solve."

For years, the education system has been about transferring knowledge. And over the past decade or so, we've gotten better at giving learners (both teachers and students) access to tools, but Brookhouser and other forward-thinking educators like him know that transfer of knowledge and even teaching people how to use technology isn't enough.

"In the past, that worked pretty well. If you gave students enough knowledge or taught them how to follow a certain set of instructions, they could go out in the world and be successful. I think that model has started to shift significantly. Education is no longer a matter of simply showing students some instructions to follow, or formulas to follow, or filling their heads up with enough knowledge. What we need to do is help them develop a mindset—one that is constantly learning, one that's able to look at a novel problem and have the courage to try to solve it."

The Power of a Permeable Classroom

One way to develop that mindset of thinking bigger and more courageously is to provide students with opportunities to experience meaningful learning in ways that have real-world connections and applications. That means we need to have permeable classrooms, settings that let *in* a little bit of the world and let *out* a little bit of what the students are doing. Connecting students with peers—in their classroom and in classrooms around the world—as well as with experts, authors, and business and community leaders has never been easier. All you need is somebody who has a smartphone out in the field, and you can connect with them on Google Hangouts or FaceTime.

In practice, a permeable classroom could allow for something as simple as having students coordinate a neighborhood cleanup. It could mean inviting experts into the classroom via video calls. It often means connecting students with opportunities outside the classroom walls as we did with the internships for students' senior projects; for example, one of my students wanted to be an astronaut and wanted exploring the final frontier to be the focus of his senior project. Honestly, my first thought was, *How do I get this kid hours as an astronaut?* He ended up visiting NASA's Jet Propulsion Laboratory at the (relatively) nearby California Institute of Technology and had the opportunity to fly a Space Shuttle simulator. It was a challenging learning experience for him; he even crashed the Space Shuttle during his final demonstration.

My point here is that a permeable classroom allows for learning beyond what typically happens in the confines of a school. We never would have even looked for a Space Shuttle simulator if he hadn't had the opportunity to choose the topic for his senior project and been challenged to find ways to get internship hours. Even when students have big or crazy ideas regarding what they want to learn, if you can find a way to take one step toward that goal and help connect them with the right people, you can find a way to make learning more meaningful.

A permeable classroom allows for learning beyond what typically happens in the confines of a school.

Another, broader example of the permeable classroom can be seen in the work at the Moonshot Laboratory in Hawaii, where students spend one day a week (20 percent of their school time) in "a hypercollaborative community center that combines the cutting-edge tools of the modern economy with an international network of experts to help students design, develop, and build moonshot solutions to the great challenges of their day." The learning network these students have access to includes a spectrum of on- and off-site educators, researchers, coders, business leaders,

GUEST VOICE: KEVIN BROOKHOUSER
REALITY-BASED LEARNING

Educator, Learning Animal, coauthor of *The 20time Project* and *Code in Every Classroom*, @brookhouser, kevinbrookhouser.com, Monterey, California

To take on a class where the emphasis is on student agency, one must give up some of the control of that class and allow for a degree of ambiguity, at best, and what appears to be chaos, at worst. That's incredibly uncomfortable for teachers, in general, because it's contrary to what they've been taught as good classroom management. There's also the fear of, *What happens when someone walks into my classroom? It's going to look like chaos!*

And sometimes it does.

But from my experience in how the real world works, and how the world and organizations of the future will work, life is really ambiguous. We don't really know exactly what is going to happen next week. When you get a job (now or in the future), there aren't that many places where a manager says, "Hey, these are the things I want you to do. Let me know when those get done, and I'll evaluate you on those things." That's just not the reality today, and it certainly won't be of the jobs of the future. So what we need is to create classrooms that are more aligned with reality.

> **If you think your only job is to transfer knowledge from your brain to your students' brains, then I think you're going to get outsourced pretty quickly.**

If you think your only job is to transfer knowledge from your brain to your students' brains, then I think you're going to get outsourced pretty quickly. But if you believe that your purpose is to provide human experiences for students to discover how they find problems that they're interested in solving and how they go about finding their own purpose, then the next step is to give them that opportunity. The truth is, it is far more fun to hand off that power to the students and really see them create something that you couldn't imagine being possible, to watch something come from nothing, with you as the teacher merely providing the conditions that allow that to happen. It's a really fun way to teach a class, and it gives me a sense of optimism in a world where I don't always feel optimistic.

A Message from the Future

There are three elements that teachers spend much of their time juggling: knowledge transfer, skills transfer, and human connection with the student. I think we're going to see the knowledge-transfer element of it start to become discounted or get outsourced; it's already happening. Skills transfer will get outsourced through virtual and augmented reality.

The one thing I don't think is going to get outsourced anytime soon—the area where we need to focus our energy—is on that human component. What makes you human, as a teacher? What's that human connection between you and your students? The quest of education is not just acquisition of knowledge, but finding one's purpose.

engineers, and more. The kids identify problems (some of them huge), dream up potential solutions, and then, with the help of educators and experts, iterate on their solutions until they are ready to share with their community or the world. Moonshot Incubator takes this model of the permeable classroom a step further by empowering and equipping students to turn their plans into start-up businesses and organizations financially backed by investors (venture capitalists, nonprofits, school districts, angel investors, and others) who help ensure some of these students' big ideas come to life on a massive scale.

Brendan Brennan, who oversees "Ground Control" at the Moonshot Incubator in Hawaii, loves to share stories of high school-aged students around the globe who are hard at work on their moonshot ideas. One of those stories is of Boyan Slat, who, at eighteen, proposed the idea of a giant ocean sweeper that collects the plastic that's floating around in the ocean. A model of Boyan's concept is out in the Pacific right now working to clean up the ocean, and studies show that the machine could remove more than 7.25 million tons of plastic from world's oceans in ten years (TheOceanCleanup.com).

Another story Brennan shares is of a group of students at his school in Honolulu who are uniting Hawaii's rich ocean-exploring history with technology. Working with an app developer, they are creating a Hawaiian star compass. Using star lines and the Hawaiian names of the stars, the app will allow sailors to wear Google Glass and see the Hawaiian star map in the sky as they navigate. In the process, he says, "They are starting to reclaim their culture, and they are seeing the opportunity in technology to spread this love for the earth and of understanding nature around the world." Although a number of schools are pushing the boundaries of traditional education by increasing student agency, their stories are still the exceptions. To change education, we must ensure that today's students are prepared for tomorrow's reality. That means they should be creating things that are meaningful to the world outside; they should be collaborating with people outside their classroom; and they should certainly be sharing their work and their solutions outside their classroom.

Overcoming the Resistance

Making the shift to a classroom or school where student agency is the norm does not happen without challenges. Common worries teachers cite are that they will end up doing too much work—or not enough. Even if they can't articulate it, some may feel that they'll lose their power or position if they aren't in control of the learning. Others think 20 percent time or inquiry-based learning sounds like a whole lot of effort—or a waste of time. In truth, finding ways to connect your students with people, agencies, and opportunities does take work. But the students are the ones who should be doing the heavy lifting. They should be doing the creating, making, and sharing—all of which are far more powerful and meaningful and memorable than sitting, listening, and regurgitating. Educators play a more meaningful role, too, at turns challenging students to stretch beyond their comfort zones, encouraging those who need it, and empowering students with new tools or strategies when they need assistance.

Kevin Brookhouser, who teaches digital citizenship and computer science, says that when he shifted to 20 percent time and project-based learning, the two groups of people that pushed back the hardest were teachers and students. Teachers were put off by the ambiguity that comes with embracing true student agency. That didn't surprise him. What did surprise him was the resistance he received from students.

"I really thought that students would immediately embrace this kind of learning environment," Brookhouser says. "I believe that people like to be free and like to have some agency over their lives; I certainly do. I thought becoming an adult and getting to make my own decisions was a great thing; I'm not a big fan of being told what to do.

"But a lot of students really do want to be told what to do, especially the higher-performing students and especially those who are further along in their schooling. Students start to figure out school. They think, *Here's what I need to do: I need to figure out what my teacher wants. I need to do that thing, and figure out what my teacher likes, and do that thing, and if I can do that effectively, then I can get the good grade that I want, and I can move on with my life.*"

GUEST VOICE: TREVOR MACKENZIE
THE POWER OF RELATIONSHIP

English Teacher, Instructional Coach, author of *Dive into Inquiry* and *Inquiry Mindset*, @trev_mackenzie, Victoria, British Columbia, Canada

Knowing my students and knowing their stories, knowing their curiosities, their passions, and their interests allows me to really help them have more ownership over their learning. Ownership over learning can be scary for some students. It could cause anxieties and uncertainties for the student and the teacher. The more I know them, the better I know how to support them, and the better I can help them explore curiosities that, when successfully explored, are going to give them confidence in having more agency over learning.

Relationship starts before I even have a student enrolled in my classroom. I'll see a student in the hallway and they're not in my classroom, and I'll give them a high-five or I'll ask them how their day is going. And then, when they're in my classroom two years later, we've already started a connection.

Make trust your learning objective. How can you create trust and a relationship with your learners? I challenge you to create a lesson plan where that is the goal of the lesson. What are you doing in a single hour with your students where you're building relationship and trust? If those are the hallmarks of learning in the classroom, our students are going be those critical thinkers, and those collaborators, and those empathetic people in society that our future needs.

A Message from the Future

Take risks in getting away from overstandardization and overprescription, and try to find the student voice in learning. Empower our students in their role in learning by giving them some voice and some choice in terms of what it is they do with their time at school in order to create authentic and relevant learning experiences.

He's right! I remember my advanced placement (AP) students telling me, "Wagner, you can't do this to us!" when given a greater degree of choice and autonomy in how they could demonstrate their understanding of classic literature.

Trevor MacKenzie, author of *Dive into Inquiry*, agrees that making the shift toward student agency can be challenging. "Our students are really accustomed to the traditional structures and models of learning that we have had them explore and experience in our educational institutions," he says. The solution is what he calls the gradual release of learning. "By going through a gradual release of learning—from the teacher to the student—we empower our students with the skills and the understandings necessary to be successful agents over learning."

Like so many things in education, that release of learning requires that educators model for students the behaviors they want to see, starting with showing students how to design their learning. "In the first few months of my courses, I model what strong lesson and unit design looks like," MacKenzie says. "We refine that metacognitive piece of learning and have the students reflect and put words to their thoughts and understandings so that they can find their own learning pathways in the future." From there, students codesign the syllabus. "I identify the must-dos and must-knows in our course work, and then everything else is open to their interests, their passions, their strengths, and how they want to grow in terms of being a learner. When we weave those together, they see that their role in our classroom is quite different than they have experienced previously. And that helps with the transition."

Increasing student agency also requires adjusting and personalizing the pace at which learning occurs. "We have to recognize that not only are students very diverse in their needs and in their understandings, but they're coming to our classrooms from other classrooms in our buildings where teachers are teaching in different ways and in different pedagogies and with different goals in mind," MacKenzie explains. "By being mindful of that transition, we can support them as we take a different learning role in our classroom—one that fosters and values agency. So transition means taking time, slowing things down a bit. So slow things down and listen to the students in your room and ask them the powerful questions about their reflections on learning."

Increasing student agency takes time, planning, and persistence. Systems and best practices like those Kevin Brookhouser espouses in his book *The 20Time Project* and that Trevor MacKenzie provides in *Dive into Inquiry* help, but the shift starts with a change of mindset (as Trevor MacKenzie addresses in his second book, *Inquiry Mindset*) and a willingness to empower students to drive their own learning.

Start Small: If asking kids what they want to learn feels too wide open, Kevin Brookhouser suggests reviewing the math, reading, and/or language arts standards with your students and asking them how they want to go about accomplishing those standards in the next three months. "Start by providing students with the opportunity to have some agency, and see how it works," he says.

Gaming to Learn

Student agency is about moving from a classroom where the teacher is the most active participant to one where the kids are the most active participants. Earlier I mentioned the resistance teachers feel toward student agency, and in some ways I can relate. It's easy for me to feel like I'm not doing my job when *I'm* not the one performing or working hard or fully engaged. But we have to get over that if we want *students* to be fully engaged. Games are a tool educators can use to engage kids in learning. One way to help transition power to students is to give them a game simulation to control. In my experience, the minute you bring games into the classroom, suddenly the kids are the busy ones instead of the teachers—which, in my philosophy, is the way it should be.

The first game my own kids, Clark and Finn, got really crazy about was Minecraft. I remember watching Finn play Minecraft on his tablet one day when he was about three. I didn't know a whole lot about the game at that point, but in the game world I could see him moving around in a house with windows, a bed, and door. So I asked, "Finn, did *you* build that?"

"Yeah," he said, moving around the in-game house.

I wasn't sure I believed him. "Finn, did you *find* that in the world?"

He said, "Nope. I built it."

"How did you make these glass windows and this bed?" I asked.

"Like this, Daddy," he said, showing me how he selected and placed the materials.

If you or your children or students have played the game, you know it's a fairly simple game to get started with, but also has a depth and complexity that can take years to master. In any case, I was floored to see that my three-year-old son had figured out how to build a house in the game without someone else teaching him how to do it.

When Finn's older brother, Clark, was in first grade, he was ready for chapter books but wasn't motivated to read them until he discovered chapter books about Minecraft. From there, a whole world of reading opened up for him. But Minecraft was the thing he was interested in—it was his gateway into more reading. It was also the gateway into learning geology. When we went hiking, Clark and Finn asked about the rocks we saw, and we discussed ores and minerals, all because of Minecraft. Later, when the boys got into *Plants Versus Zombies*, which sounded inane even to me at first, they started showing a greater interest in biology—and chess, since the video game shared strategic similarities.

Seymour Papert was famous for helping kids understand and use computers in creative ways. He was the one responsible for Logo, the educational programming language that so many of us used in school to create games when we were kids. There's a story that Papert once asked a first grader who was working on his Logo project, "How's it going?" And the first grader said, "It's hard. It's fun. It's Logo!"

Papert really dug into this idea that the kid said it was fun *because* it was hard, not in spite of it being hard. And if you think about kids and their attitudes toward video games, you can see that playing out every day. If a video game is too easy, they reject it and say, "It's boring." And obviously, if the game is too hard or too challenging, they reject it, too. Where good video games excel is in what Vygotsky called the zone of proximal development (ZPD). Good games—the games that hold players' interest and keep them trying even when their character dies—challenge players without frustrating them. Difficulty increases as the player advances, keeping them in that zone of hard fun. Additionally, if you get a really good video game, it's going to have great tutorials, or better yet, the tutorials will be built into the game world and into the story.

Educators can use the principles that make games successful, and sometimes even the games themselves, to find that sweet spot of hard and fun called *engagement*.

Applying Lessons from Games to Classrooms

Inquiry—In an open-ended game world, there are different paths to the same goal. Players can choose which quest to pursue, which path their character is going to take, and how to develop the character. There are lots of opportunities for players to make decisions and choices. This mirrors the heart of inquiry-driven learning, which provides the opportunity for students to ask questions and seek answers (in an authentic or real-world context). Inquiry-based learning is sometimes called or associated with discovery learning because, as students explore the learning context for an answer to their questions, they experience moments of discovery, which can be a powerful motivating factor. This process of posing questions and seeking answers naturally encourages students to make new connections in their mind, the essence of building schema in the constructivist philosophy. It also involves a good deal of sophisticated problem solving on the part of the student.

Social Learning—Massive Multiplayer Online Games with an open-ended world provide opportunities for social learning. Anyone who has been involved in a game like World of Warcraft, for example, knows that you can't get anything done in the game unless you collaborate with others. You're very limited in terms of what quests you could do by yourself. When you're in a group, if your clan is preparing a raid, for instance, you have to show up on time, you have to play your role, you have to stay there until it's done. Plus, you have to be flexible, communicate, and share the loot. All of those skills can be difficult to teach in a classroom, but kids are learning them in these massive multiplayer games. And the learning context is embedded. No one says, "Today we're going to learn about cooperation and group dynamics." They just play the game.

Risk Taking—One of my favorite principles of game-based learning is the psychosocial moratorium principle, which means players are able to take risks with reduced consequences. That's baked right into most games. You click around to see what things do. You try something, you fail, you try it again. Maybe you die and you have to re-spawn, but no big deal, you try it again. Being able to try again and again (and again) reduces the fear of failure. In fact, players are often willing to keep playing until they beat the level.

Problem-Solving—The way in which video games excel most is they engage students in solving problems. Often simple mobile apps and games that kids love—even those that might be about battle on the surface—amount to puzzle games.

Games don't even have to be digital to be effective. Breakout EDU is a great way to do something different in the classroom. Students learn to work together to solve clues. Depending on the game (which could focus on any subject area or grade level) and the parameters you set, students could use any number of questions and resources to solve the puzzle and open the box.

Metacognition (Analyze and Reflect)—The killer combination, it turns out, is having kids play games and then blog about it or post a video about it. Players of all ages also love to watch YouTube videos of other players doing walkthroughs in a game. So if your students are posting about gaming, they're doing so for an authentic audience. And as they watch others play, they analyze and reflect on what worked, what didn't, and why. If you are going to use games for learning in your classroom, be sure to give students a chance to reflect on what they are learning; don't miss the opportunity to encourage metacognition.

Think Like a Programmer—A popular genre of games teaches players to think like programmers. Apps like Light Bot or Apple's Swift Playgrounds are examples of games in which players move their character around by giving it instructions, writing procedures that repeat, coding conditional/if-then statements, and learning to work with variables. Similarly, block-based programming tools, like MIT's Scratch, provide an even more open-ended experience in which students can even create their own games (or try to recreate their own favorite games. Clark's recreation of Dig Dug and Finn's attempt at Super Mario Galaxy stand out in my memory). Learning to think about a problem in a systematic way, as a programmer would, can be valuable to students regardless of their future careers or pursuits.

Social Change—Learning to think like a programmer is not the only pragmatic reason for students to be engaged with video games and simulations. There are whole social movements around creating games for purposes other than entertainment. These serious games, or games for change, can play a role in educating or motivating people across many industries: the military, the scientific community, public health, emergency services, city planning, engineering, politics, and of course education. See gamesforchange.org to explore a wide variety of serious games and learn more about getting involved.

Good learning happens in the classroom the same way it does in a game, through choice, discovery, taking risks, failing, and persisting. All of those things help make a learning experience more engaging.

The constructivist philosophy is the belief that all knowledge must be actively and subjectively constructed in the mind of each individual. When the tasks required of our students have an authentic context and purpose, they take an active rather than passive role in the learning process. When we ask students what they want to learn—and provide the time, space, resources, connections, and experiences to make it possible—learning becomes meaningful because they *construct* that meaning in their minds.

36 Learning Principles of Video Games

Asking students, "What do you want to learn?" is simple, and it is the biggest gateway to getting them interested in school. Maybe they want to solve a problem that is relevant to their communities or that is related to one of their passions—it could be focused on basketball or rap or Impalas—or something seemingly impossible like being an astronaut. The topic matters far less than all the skills they'll develop in the process of inquiry, research, discovery, collaboration, and sharing. When students are excited about what they are learning, all the stuff we *have to* teach, as well as all of the tools, techniques, and technology that give them the ability to create, collaborate, and share, starts to stick. Suddenly, learning matters—to them.

"Education . . . . is empowerment to make choices and emboldens the youth to chase their dreams." **—Nita Ambani, chairperson and founder of the Reliance Foundation**

GOOGLE SEARCH: TOOLS TO HELP STUDENTS SUCCEED

Google offers a spectrum of research tools that pull from credible sites—from the most authoritative to the timeliest. Using the tools below empowers educators and students to find credible information from legitimate sources.

Google Books—Searches the world's library—tens of millions of books—and returns search terms by highlighting them in the pages of relevant books. The "My Library" feature allows users to easily curate and access titles. This is a helpful tool for librarians and teachers, who use it to curate books for students and then share a link to their digital library.

Google Scholar—Weeds out blogs and returns results from peer-reviewed journals and university publications, as well as some trade journals and magazines. Its algorithms give higher rankings to the most frequently cited papers and articles. Google Scholar also offers easy citation tools to boot—and the ability to discover studies that have cited the one you've already found.

Google News—Uses algorithms, not human editors, to pull timely content from legitimate news sources around the web and bring the most-heavily cited or interacted with to the top of the results list. This is a great place to start discussions of current events at any grade level. It's also a great tool for introducing information literacy by looking at headlines from different sources to explore the authority and authenticity of the source as well as the bias or agenda in the text.

Google Alerts—Allows users to set search terms and receive a daily email listing any new results for those search terms. This can be like having a 24/7 research team delivering new results to your inbox every morning.

Advanced Search—google.com/advanced_search helps users find exactly what they're looking for:

- Include or exclude specific phrases.

- Search for a number range (e.g., years or dollar amounts).

- Restrict a search to a particular domain, like .edu or your district website (e.g., nmusd.us).

- Refine your search by language, region, last update.

- Search for file types (e.g., PDFs, PowerPoint, or Excel files).

- Use the usage rights feature to find files, images, etc., that are free to share.

Explore and cite in Google Docs—Clicking on the Explore symbol in a Google Doc brings up a sidebar where users can search the web, Google Images, or their own drive for more resources to add to the Doc. Hovering over the source reveals a quotation symbol that, when clicked, adds a footnote citation in MLA, APA, or Chicago format.

CHAPTER FIVE
INSPIRING SPACES

The harder you fight to hold on to specific assumptions, the more likely there's gold in letting go of them.
–John Seeley Brown, organizational studies researcher

> **Inspiring Spaces are comfortable, beautiful, and flexible environments that invite students to learn by engaging their curiosity, wonder, and natural physical energy.**

At American School of Bombay elementary campus in Mumbai, you won't hear a bell to signal lunch time. In fact, there is no "bell schedule." Break times happen when the teachers notice that their students are low on energy or are getting squirrely and need to run around a bit. If lunchtime rolls around and everyone is deep into their projects, the class stays in flow and keeps working. Like the schedule, the physical learning space in this school is flexible. Rather than being composed of a bunch of small classrooms, the elementary space is large and open. Teachers and students have the freedom to rearrange partitions, bookcases, and the rest of the furniture (all of which is on wheels) as needed. Learning spaces in the upper grades are just as creative and flexible, meeting the needs of students as they work, learn, and play together. It's a school that encourages students to "Dream. Learn. Serve." Everything about the building supports that endeavor. To get a glimpse of what that looks like in action, watch the video at asbindia.org.

'Iolani School in Hawaii is another example of a school where the environment contributes to a culture of connected, student-driven learning. With a garden on the rooftop and a makerspace in the basement, the school's dedicated learning center is a place where students are inspired to create and innovate. In the previous chapter, I wrote about a few of the things students can learn from video games. Well, at 'Iolani, the students rigged up a bicycle to create electricity that powers a video-game system—combining physical activity with games and engineering. Every quarter, students redecorate the elevator. The first time I took a ride in it, the theme was *Yellow Submarine*. There was a lighting system, a sound system, and motorized 3D printed plastic cut outs—all programmed by students to enhance The Beatles theme. A few quarters later, I visited again, and the theme was Frank Sinatra. (Clearly, music is part of this school's culture!) Check out what's going on at this impressive school at iolani.org.

Learning spaces should reflect the culture you want in your classroom or school. If you want kids sitting in rows listening to lectures, then the traditional spaces are arguably effective. But if you want to take a different approach to learning, the spaces in your school need to look different from a traditional classroom. They should be comfortable, beautiful, and flexible enough to meet the needs of your learners while inspiring them to explore their passions and use their curiosity, wonder, and physical energy. The typical classroom is none of those things. It's not comfortable; students sit in metal chairs with weird wooden desks in front of them. Unless the teacher has gone to great effort, the classrooms are not beautiful—most schools look like brick boxes. The traditional industrial, uncomfortable metal furniture doesn't add to the beauty, nor is it flexible.

If you want to take a different approach to learning, the spaces in your school need to look different from a traditional classroom.

Typically, teachers organize students in rows and lecture to them from the front of the room. But if you are able to do something that purposely breaks from those conventions, you can create an environment that kids want to learn in. That changes everything. As Loris Malaguzzi writes in *The Third Teacher*, "There are three teachers of our children: adults, other children, and their physical environment."

What Do Your Learning Spaces Say about Your School's Culture?

Designing inspiring spaces begins with identifying what you want your school culture to be. That's why one of the first questions David Jakes asks when he first visits a school as a design consultant is, "Can you give me a document that presents your expectations and desires for the student learning experience?" Most of the time, he says, "They can't, because they haven't defined it." While curriculum and learning goals certainly contribute to the design, the way you want students to feel when they walk into the building and the kinds of interaction they have—with each other and with the space itself—are equally important. Culture goes beyond the mission statement, which, as Jakes points out, tends to be very similar from school to school: "'In our district, we value life-long learning and helping students become productive members to society.' It's the same thing over and over. But when I'm working with a school to design or redesign spaces, I'm looking for something that is deeper. My role is to push them to quantify the learning experience."

Whether redesigning an entire school or a single classroom, creating a makerspace, or developing a multipurpose library space, when school leaders and educators think of purchasing new furniture or redesigning learning spaces, the focus is generally on making improvements to what the school is already doing. Any progress toward spaces that are more comfortable, beautiful, and flexible is a step in the right direction, but that kind of focus may not be enough—because what traditional schools are doing now isn't enough to equip students with the kinds of technical, innovative,

GUEST VOICE: DAVID JAKES
LOOKING BEYOND COLLEGE AND CAREER READINESS
Chief Design Officer, David Jakes Designs,
@djakes, DavidJakesDesigns.com,
Naperville, Illinois

Schools typically prepare kids for three trajectories: going to college, going to work, or going into the military. But what's beyond that? Where in schools right now are they preparing kids for an entrepreneurial cycle—where they create their own careers and their own place in the world? School is not about college and career readiness. We all know, as adults with experience, that where you end up is a lot different than the places you anticipated. Education is about becoming prepared for the pathway of life and what that means in terms of having the skills to be adaptive, responsive, and anticipatory. It's also about empathy. We tend to lose sight of this given the velocity of our world today.

Kids need advocates. Kids need adults. Kids need human beings to work with them. It's even more true today than it was ten years, even five years ago. That need for influence will only increase. Let's focus on relationships and developing empathy. We're going to need that in a world that has the tendency to spin out of control at any moment.

A Message from the Future

Will your students have the ability to understand their opportunities, manage their choices, and take advantage of them? How will you use technology, spaces, and human beings to help kids become literate in a new and expansive way that allows them to create themselves into existence and project to the world what they know, what they think, and what they can do? Think differently; think more boldly; make no little plans.

and, in particular, the collaborative and interpersonal skills they will need in the future. If learning can happen anywhere, then, as David Jakes points out, "School is just a single space in a larger place of learning." Free access to information has significantly changed learning—both in how we learn and the skills and knowledge we need to acquire—so it only makes sense that our learning spaces should change as well. Our goal must be to design schools and classrooms that promote learning and connection—spaces that allow for collaboration, for reflection, for discovery, and for creation.

Comfortable

One of the most common complaints students have concerning their learning spaces is that they are physically uncomfortable. "Once you get over the hump of making them comfortable, then you have a fighting chance of teaching them something," David Jakes says.

"Where do you learn best?" Rebecca Hare, a teacher, design consultant, and coauthor of *The Space*, asks this question every time she does a workshop for teachers. "Most teachers respond that they work in the kitchen on a stool with a big surface area. A lot of teachers sit on the couch with a pillow on their lap, their laptop on top of it. There are very few teachers who actually go and sit at a desk at home to do their work."

We all learn best when we're comfortable—when our backs don't hurt and our legs aren't cramped and we have plenty of space for our book or tablet or laptop or paper. Why then do schools confine students to small, cramped desks with hard seats and very little room to write, create, or use a Chromebook or iPad? "It's like a little prison," Hare says. "Creating more comfortable environments that mimic the way we sit and move when we are learning independently can help spark that kind of natural learning in our kids during the school day."

Comfortable learning spaces might have exercise balls or standing desks or bean bags or pillows or couches. What they won't have are rows and rows of small, isolating, and *uncomfortable* desks.

What can you do to make your learning spaces more comfortable?

Beautiful

Beautiful, interesting, and creative spaces invite students to learn. At Singapore American School, Ron Starker, a librarian and the author of *Transforming Libraries*, creates homey spaces with comfort and functionality built in. He and his team created archetypal learning environments, drawing from David Thornberg's *Campfires in Cyberspace* to improve the learning experience in the library:

- **The Campfire**—Couches and chairs are arranged for group discussions.

- **The Watering Hole**—An informal gathering space where people can snack and share ideas.

- **The Cave**—A quiet space where students can work in solitude.

- **The Mountaintop**—Designed to accommodate large audiences, this space is equipped with sound, lighting, and a projection system.

Additionally, the Singapore American School's library includes spaces such as the **Living Room**, which brings in elements of nature (including plants and a large tiger representing the school's mascot). It also has a **recording studio**, **reading room**, **design center**, **photography studio**, **wellness zone**, and a place for solitude called **pier point**, equipped with pod chairs that cut down on distractions.

Beautiful spaces engage the mind as well as the body. Not unlike a Google office with bikes and nap pods, we can design learning spaces that take into account that students—humans—are not little central processing units. Putting kids in a grove in the woods (even if the "woods" are in your classroom) lets them learn in an environment more conducive to reflection and creativity. (Explore the Japanese concept of forest bathing for more on the psychological and physiological benefits of being in the woods.)

When spaces are designed with purpose, they can be both beautiful and functional. In classrooms, beauty could mean adding "Easter eggs"—fun finds for students, including questions, prompts, or interesting quotes on the walls. In my son's fourth-grade classroom, the teacher has an easel just outside the room where she posts interesting facts and images designed to engage students' natural curiosity and wonder before they even come into the class.

What can you do to add beauty to your learning spaces?

Flexible

If you go to a nice hotel or a modern airport, you'll see flexible and varied spaces. You can sit in the lounge chair and rest or read. If you want to work, you sit or stand at a high table while charging your device. Wi-Fi is ubiquitous. There are play areas for families so young children can stop and unleash pent-up energy, and there are cozy spots for sitting and talking. The same should be true of schools because flexible, varied spaces in schools contribute to better learning.

Flexible is a broad term that encompasses the idea that our learning spaces—and everything in them—must respond to different needs of those using them.

- Do we need a full-group space?
- Do we need to be able to break out into small teams?
- Do we need to be able to pair up?
- Do we need to be able to move all this stuff out of the way so that we can use our bodies and move in this space?

Those are all elements of flexibility.

Some of my favorite examples of flexible learning spaces are schools where all the furniture is on wheels: chairs, tables, bookshelves, screens, interactive whiteboards or panels, projectors—everything. Sometimes even the walls have wheels. In these flexible open-concept schools, teachers can create learning spaces as needed.

Flexibility can also refer to the tech capabilities in the space. Do you have one big screen at the front of the room, or smaller screens that kids can plug into? Maybe you just use a Chromecast that allows everybody to take turns up front. Something as simple as a forty-dollar Chromecast can add flexibility to the learning environment.

Guest Voice: Rebecca Hare
Space to Collaborate

Teacher, Design Consultant, and coauthor of *The Space,*

@RLH_DesignED, rlh-designed.weebly.com,

Miami, Florida

If I want my kids to be collaborative and work together, I don't give them a letter-sized piece of paper that's designed for one person. When we start a group project, I don't hand them one sheet of paper with the instructions, because the person who is holding the paper is now in charge. They're automatically the leader, and no one else can read the paper.

If you want to have a whole group collaborating, you need to have them on a surface that supports all of the people. That's where whiteboard walls or giant pieces of paper come into play. I give everyone a different colored dry-erase marker and write the problems or questions where everyone can see them. Then the kids go to work, writing on the walls or big pieces of paper. And here's the benefit for me as the teacher: **I can step back, look at the wall, and see who has contributed. I can evaluate whether somebody was being marginalized in the group, and I can check for understanding and see what everybody is thinking because I know the students by the color of their marker.** Then I can photograph their work and use that for assessment.

Surfaces and surrounding can really change the way kids work. A lot of trendy, beautiful new furniture for classrooms has these tiny surfaces that are just perfect if you have a laptop. But if we want our kids really collaborating, individual surfaces won't work.

> A lot of trendy, beautiful new furniture for classrooms has these tiny surfaces that are just perfect if you have a laptop.
> But if we want our kids really collaborating, individual surfaces won't work.

A Message from the Future

What is the legacy you are leaving with your learners every single day? So often, teachers are content focused, but we know that the kids aren't going to remember the content. Instead, if you're teaching history, how can you switch to teaching students to think like a historian? If you're teaching art, how can you make it less about an artist or a process, and more about teaching students to behave as artists?

When kids can learn the thinking patterns and really own them, you're leaving a legacy with them of continued learning and engagement. It doesn't matter if they forget when a war was or a certain math fact. If they can engage in learning and life like a mathematician or writer, a scientist and a historian, then I think we've done a good job with them.

And just like the space should reflect the culture, the culture impacts the way we teach, learn, and use the space. "I run creative spaces and makerspaces and my students have total autonomy within those spaces," Rebecca Hare says. "They learn where the tools are and how to use them. So I'm not obsessed with flexible seating because the kids are the flexible elements in my space. If they have to use a laser cutter, they go over to the laser cutter. If they need to use the sinks, or work on the floor . . . wherever they need to work they have the freedom to move and use the space in a way that best suits them."

What can you do to make your learning spaces flexible enough to meet your learners' needs?

Tips to Make Your Learning Spaces Inspiring

"Your learning space is one of the vital tools educators need to use, when designing learning experiences for kids," Hare says. It's not arbitrary, and it will affect the way that students learn, how they engage, how they collaborate and how they eventually begin to own their own learning. When teachers can leverage that, it can really unleash a different kind of learning for kids."

Ask the Stakeholders—Engage students, teachers, and community members in the process of designing the learning spaces. Find out what's most important for them and what the drivers are for the larger school community. Do they really want to focus on collaboration, do they want to focus on innovation, do they want to focus on tradition?

Consider Form *and* Function—Yellowknife is a mining community in Canada. When building a new school, the stakeholders wanted the space to have a community feel that reflected the area's tradition. With that in mind, the design included a commons area—known as the "gathering stairs"—that incorporates exposed rock. In this really cool space where students congregate, they are reminded of the larger community's roots.

Keep It Flexible—Tanya Avrith, coauthor of *The Google Infused Classroom*, had a budget of $2,500 to redesign her classroom in a school just outside Montreal, Canada. That wouldn't buy all new furniture for the room, so she got creative. The woodshop students designed arched desks that fit together in different configurations. She painted the walls white and hung shower boards (great white board spaces), and added a flat-screen monitor. Oh, and she brought in a coffee maker. The room, affectionately dubbed the "white room," is where students hang out during breaks, lunch, and after school. Tanya's no longer at that school, and it's still one of the students' most popular spaces.

Encourage Connections—In most schools today, the classrooms and other learning spaces remain disconnected. "Right now, if you go through the halls with classrooms on each side, you see that kids, even within their classrooms, are fairly isolated," David Jakes says. "You see them sitting in rows. You see them not being able to talk to the person next to them. Creating inspiring spaces requires that we end the isolation that's inherent within individual classrooms and design spaces that engage kids, promote community, and intentionally create connections." Inspiration is often born of connection with others' ideas and perspectives.

> **"Creating inspiring spaces requires that we end the isolation that's inherent within individual classrooms and design spaces that engage kids, promote community, and intentionally create connections."**

Consider Seating (and Standing)—Changing the posture of your students alters how they learn. "You can change their level of engagement when you understand the way posture affects learning" Rebecca Hare says. "If we want our kids collaborating, they should probably be on stools leaning in, engaging with people. They could be standing in the hallway or sitting around in a circle, but they should be leaning in. That leaning-in body language tells your collaborators you are engaged, and it kind of forces engagement."

In contrast, she says traditional chairs and desks promote *dis*engagement. "If you put kids in chairs with backs on them, they're going to naturally lean back. Their bottoms are going to scoot forward, and they get into more of a reflective pose. That's a great thing for reading or for independent reflection, but it's not great for conversation and collaboration."

"Once you start to make these transformations in your space and the kids start to have more agency, they get excited because they finally get to have a say in their environment," Hare says. Working and learning in inspiring spaces inevitably leads to pedagogical changes. "It's really hard to make great pedagogical changes if you're not going to change your space. And it's really hard to change your space and not change pedagogy. The two things are really done in tandem."

Does Your Learning Space Need Some Redesign?

- What is the first thing students and visitors see as they approach your building?
- As you walk into your classroom or school, does it feel like a home?
- Does your building feel clinical, like a doctor's office?
- Does your space promote community or isolation?
- Can you see student work on display?
- Do students work well in groups?
- Does the teacher stand at the front of the room?
- Could you spend the day sitting where your students sit all day?
- Can you access Wi-Fi from anywhere in the building?
- Are there quiet spaces for reflection?
- Are you spaces *over*designed or visually cluttered?

MAKING EVERYONE FEEL AT HOME IN THE LIBRARY (OR ANYWHERE IN YOUR SCHOOL)

Depending upon your school community's needs and interests, you could create a wide variety of zones, studios, and learning spaces within your library, school, or classroom. While schools tend to be improving their overall look, most still have an institutional feel, with fluorescent lighting, conservative structural designs, and standardized furnishings. But considerable brain-based research is being done and much of it points toward the idea that homelike environments tend to promote learning. Homey layouts encourage interaction, comfortable furniture reduces stress, bright colors stimulate the brain, seating arrangements foster face-to-face conversations, and immersive settings allow hands-on experiences.

Perhaps educational institutions should look and feel more like a family home, a Silicon Valley office, a nice hotel, or an exotic resort. I don't believe we need to suffer in bad environments to learn; rather, we learn best when we feel safe, comfortable, and at home. And, as we say at EdTechTeam, learning can be fun, so the same can be true of our spaces.

Agile or Purpose-Built?

When we look at improving a learning space, we always have to consider the stakeholders' unique needs. For example, libraries for young children will need to be more concerned with safety, whereas those serving older students should provide adequate access to technology. One of the ways we can identify our learners' needs is to simply ask them how they learn best:

Do you work best in small groups or on your own?

Do you fall asleep when you read on a pillow, or do you really get into the story better when you are more comfortable?

Then observe.

As we go up the educational ladder, library studios for subjects such as videography and photography or music need to be purpose-built. Other areas can be more flexible and agile, allowing for a wider spectrum of activities to support several types of learning.

Case in point: Musicians perform best in purpose-built concert halls that take acoustics, seating, and experience-enhancing aesthetics into account. Artists work best in art studios that have proper lighting, allow for adventurous experimentation, and are equipped with proper brushes, canvases, and paints. And in the same vein, students tend to learn best in comfortable areas that allow for innovation and creativity, as well as collaboration, communication, and critical thinking.

—Adapted from Transforming Libraries by Ron Starker

CHAPTER SIX
ROBUST INFRASTRUCTURE

We build too many walls, and not enough bridges.
–Isaac Newton

> ## Robust Infrastructure is the technology, networks, hardware, and other resources (including policy) that make deeper experiences possible without detracting from the learning.

Just as inspiring spaces shape and support a school's culture, a robust infrastructure supports the learning that happens in the school. Technology and the infrastructure that enables it—from the devices to the networks to the cloud—are vital to modern education. But it's something that few educators ponder on a daily basis unless something isn't working in their classrooms or schools. And to some extent, that's okay. If the job of technology is to support learning, it should *seamlessly* support instruction. Teachers should not have to think about whether the internet is going to work in their classroom or wonder if the computer or program they want to use will start on command. Nor should an educator have to spend time logging in, putting a password in the filter, calling the IT technician, or fiddling with the projector. When those things happen during instructional time, technology becomes a distraction (just like that pencil sharpener grinding in the background). Students and teachers should be able to open their devices and get to work—without "technical difficulties." The only thing teachers should have to think or wonder about concerning technology is how to use it to amplify their lessons, make learning experiences meaningful, and make student thinking visible. The technology itself should simply work, and that doesn't happen by accident.

Technical support personnel must prioritize the needs of students.

All too often, the infrastructure and the people who are responsible for it act as barriers to the learning that should be happening in the school. It's not like they're stealing textbooks out of kids' hands, but they sometimes make it harder for students to access and use the most important resources and tools. Case in point:

A few years ago, EdTechTeam donated a class set of Chromebooks to a middle school where a 1:1 student-to-computer ratio wasn't yet a reality. After a great deal of resistance from the district's IT department, they finally agreed that the teacher and students could use the Chromebooks— but not for Google Docs! This was a largely (but by no means entirely) Windows-based district, and the blatant obstructionism was driven by fear and a territorial response rather than what was best for the students in the classroom. Eventually, with additional pressure from the teacher and school leaders, the IT department relented. But even then, the hoops they made the teacher jump through (for student usernames and for Wi-Fi access) were unnecessary obstacles to learning on a daily basis. This sort of scenario is still surprisingly common in schools.

To be fair, I have seen and can empathize with both sides of these conflicts. I understand why IT departments want to standardize and scale their operations on a limited budget. I also know many IT professionals who work heroically to make technology seamless and reliable for students. Some heroic technology directors, like Mark Garrison and Jennie Magiera, even appear in this book.

Technical support personnel must prioritize the needs of students. They must also be willing to consider the needs, skills, and abilities of the educators they are serving, because when you make changes without thinking, progress can feel like a step backward. Just before I took a position as a district level education technology coordinator at the Newport-Mesa Unified School District (in 2004), the district applied for and received a grant to put 1,200 handheld devices (Palm Pilots) into the hands of middle schoolers. The idea was that having students use these devices in their language arts and social studies classes would allow teachers to measure and show growth as the students wrote on the devices. But when administrators applied for the grant, *they gave little thought to the teachers who were going to be involved.* When I came on board, part of my job was to roll out the implementation of these handhelds. In the two schools where the grant was implemented, the most resistant and least tech-savvy teachers happened to be in the language arts and social studies departments. Regardless of the goals of the grant, these were the wrong people for an early 1:1 pilot. My biggest takeaway from this project was realizing how little thought was given to the individuals involved. Many of them were nearing retirement and wanted nothing to do with the program. One woman in particular happened to have only one hand—and the devices had a stylus requiring two-handed use. There was no consideration given to the fact that she was one of the language arts teachers identified for the focus of the grant. She felt unseen (and insulted) and wanted nothing to do with the devices.

When it comes to integrating technology into education, teachers may not share the same vision for learning as their leaders; they may not even know what the vision is. Not everyone understands *how* to use technology in ways that move education forward. Fearful parents and stretched IT coordinators fight one-to-one devices or internet access. Furthermore, antiquated programs and infrastructure can't keep pace with current technology and learning demands. Funding, policies, and people can make it challenging to integrate technology in schools. That's where a clear vision, a well-developed plan, and good communication come into play.

Vision

"You can delegate implementation, but the vision for the way technology will transform learning has to rest with the school or district leadership," says Richard Culatta, CEO of ISTE. Before moving to ISTE, Richard served as the chief innovation officer (CIO) for the state of Rhode Island and led the office of education technology at the U.S. Department of Education. He believes that leaders must take responsibility for driving the vision for technology, even as they work *with* their CIO or chief technology officer (CTO) to see the vision brought to reality. Having heard superintendents and school principals abdicate that responsibility on the grounds of not being "tech-savvy," he pushes leadership to step up or step aside.

Maybe that sounds harsh, but you wouldn't go to a doctor who refused to use the best technology available because he likes old-school medicine. Nor would you want to get in a plane flown by a pilot who refuses to learn how to use technology when every modern plane today is essentially a flying computer. "A pilot who says, 'I'm not comfortable with that newfangled tech' should not be flying," Richard says. "I believe the same is true with school leadership. That doesn't mean that I want a superintendent to be a database administrator. It doesn't mean that I want leaders implementing or being administrators of these systems. It *does* mean that the vision for how technology is going to be used cannot be delegated."

Of course, smart leaders pull in teachers, their CIO or CTO, and other experts from without and within the organization to help build the vision for the role of technology in the school or district. As Richard notes, the leader doesn't have to know how to implement the tech; however, he or she should be intentional about discovering what the possibilities are for technology in education. Listening to those expert voices, attending conferences and workshops to learn about how technology can open doors for improved learning, and being a connected educator can help you craft the vision for your school.

As you work to develop or refine your vision and shape your technology plan, start by answering a few questions about the kind of learning you want to see in your classrooms, how to support educators as they implement that learning, what kind of technology and funding you'll need, and how you'll know if your plan is working.

What Do You Want Teachers and Students to Do in the Classroom?

Often, as people consider how to bring technology into schools, the questions focus on hardware and networks: What processors should the computers have? How much RAM do they need? How do we get the network to reach all the buildings or classrooms? And people still go there: What device is best for our students? Should we use iPads or Chromebooks or Macbooks? And what about those new Windows devices?

But as important as those decisions are, they aren't the first questions to ask regarding technology in schools. The first question must always be: What do we want the students doing? Remember, technology's main purpose is to support the learning you want to see happening in schools. Do you want your students creating or collaborating—or both? Maybe you want them coding. Maybe you want them making.

The learning objectives for your district, school, and even within the individual classrooms should drive decisions relating to devices, tools, and infrastructure; for example, if you want kids creating and collaborating with their peers locally and globally, using the web and all it has to offer, a full browser on a cheap Chromebook is the way to go. But if you want students to have the best tools for creating audio and video, then maybe iPads or Macs may be the tools best suited for those tasks. That said, web-based tools like Soundtrap and WeVideo make Chromebooks attractive for audio and video today—*if* you have the pipeline out to the web. So the first thing to consider as you develop your technology plan is the kind of learning you want to see happening in your school or district.

Then consider what you might need to make that happen—and what you already have access to. Only then should you consider purchasing decisions.

When Tim Lee and Peter Henrie, cofounders of Amplified IT, consult with schools, the questions they ask revolve around creating an environment that supports the kind of learning and curriculum goals the teachers want to achieve in the classroom. "We want to be able to build an approach that is going to support students' learning—whether that's by leveraging Chrome devices or BYOD [bring your own device] or anything else," says Lee. The first focus isn't the device, network, or program; it's the desired outcome.

- *What do you want teachers and students to do in the classroom?*
- *What are the learning objectives for your school?*

What Kind of PD Is Necessary to Make That Learning Happen?

Determining which devices and what capabilities are necessary for your school starts when you identify your curriculum objectives—your vision for the learning experience. From there, the next question to ask focuses on empowering teachers: *What kind of professional development is necessary to make that learning happen?* Building a robust infrastructure includes offering well-balanced professional development that supports educators as they use the technology to achieve the school and district learning goals.

As the Director of Technology and Innovation at Minnesota's White Bear Lake Area Schools, Mark Garrison keeps three clear objectives in mind regarding the role of technology in his district: improved student outcomes, lower hurdles for people (students and staff), and bias toward action.

"We try to make the entry into technology really easy for people. In terms of empowering leaders and teachers, we give them tools that help them be more efficient so they can be more creative in their approach to their work," Mark says. "And when educators bring great ideas to the table, we help them make their vision a reality. It's really easy to intellectualize our work and sit around and talk about it. We're educators; we like the research part, and it can be easy to get lost in that sometimes. Instead, we are intentional to move toward action and to say, 'Let's just go ahead and try it.'"

Part of that action is providing training and support, which ties in with the goal of lowering hurdles. The district has a well-organized tech support model that includes top-tier tech administrators all the way down to students who help keep the infrastructure and devices working smoothly. "We also have an instructional support model with digital learning specialists," he says. These specialists focus on teaching educators how to use technology in their classrooms. In the process of developing the instructional support model, Mark and his team evaluated both the existing needs and what the district's goals were in terms of technology integration and learning goals for their students. With an eye on the future, they added four digital learning specialists (for a total of six) to serve the district's 625 teachers.

"When we switched to this model, where now we have six digital learning specialists, we asked, 'What would it look like if we designed a program that targets that middle 70 percent of teachers—not those high-end innovators who are going to try everything right when it comes out and not the detractors who are not ready for the pedagogical shift required to fully integrate technology—but everyone else?'"

Capturing the interests of and educating teachers about what tech can do for them and their students became the focus for Garrison's team. "Our support is structured around helping those teachers move forward," he says. Each of the digital learning specialists has a caseload of teachers with whom they check in regularly. They help teachers integrate technology into their classrooms and lesson plans in engaging and effective ways, and they support teachers through hardware and software rollouts. "We've try to roll things out in a way that makes teachers feel like the tech is supportive of their structures and what they're doing, instead of feeling like it is just another thing to learn or add on top of what they're already doing."

GUEST VOICE: JENNIE MAGIERA
START SMALL, GO SLOWLY

Chief Program Officer, EdTechTeam,

author of *Courageous Edventures*,

@MsMagiera, about.me/jenniemagiera, Chicago, Illinois

It's okay to start small. When you're building physical infrastructure, you could shut down the entire building, rewire the whole thing, and stop school for a year. Or you could do it one classroom at a time, after school and on the weekends, without disrupting things or creating stress and chaos unnecessarily.

When you're building the infrastructure mindset, instead of shutting everything down and saying, "Everybody quit your job for a year. We're going to go on a tech retreat and learn how to use technology," we say, "Let's do one room of theory at a time."

In my district, we started by learning how to check email. We had entire days where we taught people how to put Gmail on their phone. We had a workshop on notifications and one on signature lines. We went through one thing at a time, so we could really differentiate it. Because we started the first room of thought so slowly, it gave people a level of confidence around changing their mindset. Suddenly people realized, *I got through that and didn't die. Maybe I can do the next one a little bit better.*

We started with something so crazily basic, and other tech people made fun of us, saying, "You're starting with email, and you're spending two months on it?!" But starting small and going slowly paid off, and we were able to accelerate the growth and change because of that.

A Message from the Future

When you hit a wall, and you're trying to meet a goal, the wall is in your head. The wall isn't really there.

When you realize that the wall is a mindset, not a physical barrier, you'll find out you can really stretch the limits of what you're able to do for your kids.

The professional development and support offered at White Bear Lake Schools addresses technical skills as well as mindset. "Innovating your pedagogical practice around technology is more of a mindset than a skill set. When we expanded the one-to-one, or now that we're adding flat-screen displays in the classrooms, we try to use those infusions of technology as opportunities to help teachers advance their pedagogical practice." Changing the ways teachers inspire learning—from lecture style to a more collaborative and participatory style of learning—is a significant shift. As teachers in Mark's schools work with the digital learning specialists, he says, "We examine how they're using their spaces, how they're teaching, and how they're planning group work. We want to use technology integration as a chance to move away from direct instruction and toward more collaborative work."

Jennie Magiera, the former Chief Information Officer for Des Plaines Public School District 62 and current Chief Program Officer for EdTechTeam, says that ongoing professional development and tech education can empower teachers (and as a byproduct, students) to develop a sort of "muscle memory" when it comes to how technology can be used in everyday life. "People need to be aware of how they use technology, not only at school but in all environments," she says. That muscle memory, as she calls it, means that if you are having a conversation at lunch and someone tells you about a tool that you want to remember, you grab your phone and set a reminder to check it out. "Using technology should be baked into the way we think, as part of our culture," Jennie Magiera says. That comes from training and regular exposure and experience.

"Robust infrastructure," Magiera says, "is often misunderstood as electricity and carts, but I think it's a lot more. I think it's mindset, and availability." That's why, before we talk specific tools and networks and cost, we have to understand how technology can be used—both the potential for its use and its practical application. Professional development that addresses pedagogy that naturally integrates technology, the necessary tech skills, and the kind of mindset required to try new things helps ensure that whichever tools or tech systems you bring into your school environment will support the learning rather than be a distraction from it.

One more note on professional development: It isn't only for education leaders or teachers. The IT people at schools need ongoing training and exposure to new technology to stay current on advances and possibilities. "Technical teams don't get as much of that," Pete Henrie notes. "We fight, as a company, to provide professional development to the technical side of the house so those teams are learning and embracing new technologies as well." The goal, he says, is to "teach tech to the techs so their lives are easier and their teachers' and students' lives are better."

- *What kind of professional development is necessary to empower your teachers and staff to make your vision for learning a reality?*
- *How can you support teachers regarding tech skills?*
- *How can you support teachers in developing a new mindset about technology integration?*
- *What PD opportunities are available for your IT teams?*

What Tools and Infrastructure Do You Need?

We could talk next about what's popular or exciting right now in tools, but what's hot today may be surpassed by tomorrow's iteration or innovation. EdTechTeam, Google, Apple, ISTE, and other organizations regularly provide workshops to introduce and train on the latest and greatest tools and applications. But as we're sharing messages from the future, I want provide you with a few principles that can empower you to make the best decisions regarding technology integration for your school or district—whether you're reading this book in 2018 or 2028.

A Digitally Immersive Environment

One-to-one classrooms are becoming more common, but there is still a separation between digital learning and "the real world." The future is rushing at us, and all indications are that technology will only become more a part of our everyday lives. That's the kind of world for which we need to prepare our students.

GUEST VOICE: MARK GARRISON
ASK THE RIGHT QUESTIONS

Director of Technology and Innovation, White Bear Lake Area Schools, @markgarrison, markgarrison.com, Minneapolis, Minnesota

Part of my work is asking good questions and challenging people to move forward with information. Especially at a district leadership level, it's really easy to see data come in, or see a problem arise, talk about it for a while, and then feel like, "Okay, we had a good discussion about this, let's move on to the next thing," instead of asking, "What's our actionable work?" I think if you're going to be a courageous leader, you have to take action.

One of our digital learning specialists this year spent 20 percent of his time setting up maker spaces at every elementary school. These maker spaces include essential tools such as scissors, glue guns, LEGOs, Makey Makey kits, Spheros, drills, hammers, art supplies, and more that students need to create. He's got some more expensive tools that he is going to travel with to meet specific student needs, like a drone, a GoPro, and some android tablets.

We spent this past year talking, thinking, and asking questions about his plan. Before he deploys the project, he wants to make sure he has considered every hurdle that teachers are going to face in using these tools. He wants to track with them as they rethink how they're teaching and what their philosophy is in the classroom as well as how they're going to integrate the tools. That's pretty fun. It's a fun problem to have, and a good check on our bias-toward-action viewpoint. We want to get this thing out there, but we also want to make sure that we do this in a way that teachers can immediately grab onto and can't dismiss right away. That means asking the right questions first.

A Message from the Future

Find creative ways to personalize learning for every student. Technology is great, but it's only powerful insofar as it's empowering students individually. I think the more we can personalize learning for every kid, the better.

Jennie Magiera puts it this way: "Technology isn't a field trip. In the past, you would take a field trip to the computer lab and then you would go back to your environment of analog. When I moved into a leadership role, I wanted to create environments where the technology was readily available at any time, where it was part of the natural environment of learning."

If we are going to create authentic learning experiences and teach students the tech, thinking, and application skills they need (and may already be using), we must change our environments and make tools constantly available to teachers and students. "When I think about robust infrastructure, it's more than putting devices in the hands of kids. My goal is to make technology a natural and organic part of the learning environment so that students and teachers can get at it anytime—wherever they are. That is pervasive beyond the classroom. That means when they're at lunch, they can use devices; they can use them at recess and at home. It means that technology is part of their natural habitat. It's not a field trip, because everywhere you go, it's ubiquitous."

Internet Access—Everywhere

"The internet is the most important feature in an IT plan," Tim Lee says. "If you had a school that did not have desks and chairs but had internet, you'd still have an effective classroom."

A robust infrastructure ensures that internet access is available in every room of the school—and in every area of the school grounds. To that end, Jennie Magiera says, "I really fought to have Wi-Fi routers put in both the hallways and the classrooms, which a lot of people would say is a waste of money." Her reasoning has to do with the learning goals at her district's schools, which included creating flexibility in the way spaces are used. "Less and less are kids just sitting at their desks all day just looking at the front of the room," she explains. "They're going to move around, they're going to be in the hallways, and sometimes they'll all be in one space working collaboratively. We need radio bands and placement of devices that allows for agile movement throughout the classrooms."

Jennie's district also pushed the Wi-Fi outside, which isn't typical. Doing so allows for learning to continue outside. As you consider your learning goals, consider how you want to use the spaces in your school. Get advice on how to make sure internet access is available and fast so students and staff have access everywhere on campus, factoring in the effects of the physical structures, the number of people in each room, and the number of devices that may be in use at any given time.

Access to the online world isn't optional in education; it's essential. As Pete Henrie says, "Internet connection is like lights now; it's like power. And as important as it is in this day and age, it's only going to get more important moving forward because so much technology is going to be based in the Cloud."

Access to the online world isn't optional in education; it's essential.

Free and Cloud-Based Platforms

In addition to good internet connectivity, Peter Henrie and Tim Lee strongly advocate for the use of Google's G Suite for education. "The majority of schools to date simply have been replacing desktops or infrastructure or wireless, and they don't think anew," Tim says. "The change that's happened with all the Cloud computing and with what Google has brought to the frame gives a lot more opportunity for innovation to occur. It is bringing down the price points and allowing schools to innovate in many different ways."

"The classroom has expanded from just a school," Henrie adds. "It's now at Starbucks. It's now at home." Using G Suite and Cloud-based platforms allows schools to expand without the associated costs of expansion. Which is why, when Tim and Pete consult with schools, they look for ways to make the most of technology budgets and learning opportunities by leveraging Google's platform. "Schools generally have archaic systems in place, which are very cumbersome, but now you can reimagine those

A Message from the Future

From: Peter Henrie, Cofounder, Amplified IT, @AmplifiedIT, AmplifiedIT.com

Focus on moving your technology to the Cloud. Let someone else who does it better, who does it more securely, whose hardware is better than yours, deal with that part of the technology, and you focus on pushing that technology forward within your school and getting it deeper into other parts of the school.

using G Suite, a very lightweight solution which saves both money and time," Lee says. "The cost savings you can have from moving your infrastructure up to the cloud, or using services like Gmail and Drive for storage, should go back to paying for better Internet connectivity."

With platforms that are (mostly) free for education, Google's platform offers a significant cost savings and provides an appealing ability to reprioritize funds. But cost isn't the only benefit. With Cloud-based tools, schools don't need a room for servers that need to be constantly monitored. "Google's platform is constantly innovating; it's constantly changing and improving without the IT staff having to monitor, spend time, and develop or patch an update," Tim Lee says. That means IT staff can focus on supporting the instructional side of education technology, serving teachers as the digital learning specialists like they do in Mark Garrison's district.

Before you outline your school's technology and infrastructure needs, take inventory of what you have and how those things are being used. Determine the current state of your hardware, software, infrastructure, and technical support. Then identify what is necessary to implement your vision. Sometimes you can implement a good deal of your vision using what you have without the need for anything new, and sometimes evaluation reveals where you need to be spending your money going forward.

- *What is already working in your school in terms of technology?*
- *What resources do you have access to now?*
- *What tools or systems do you need to support the kind of learning you want to see in your school or district?*
- *What could using a Cloud-based platform, like Google's G Suite, make possible for your students and staff?*

How Will You Monitor Progress and Evaluate Effectiveness?

Once you have gotten all the way to the point where you have a meaningful plan, you have identified what training and tools you need. It's important to create a plan for monitoring and evaluation. Often, the strength of this aspect of your plan helps convince the powers that be to provide the funding you need to bring your plan to fruition. Part of your plan for building a robust infrastructure is to make sure your learning objectives are achieved. So ask, *How will we know if what we're doing is effective? How will we measure success?*

Set benchmarks so you and your teachers will know if you nailed it— or missed the mark. Sometimes, you'll do everything you set out to do, but the test scores stay the same, or you don't see the great projects you wanted to see from students, or the teachers continue to lecture from the front of the room. Create a plan to monitor and evaluate progress so you know where to make changes to the PD you're providing or to the way the tools are used by teachers and students.

What Funding Do You Need?

When you have a clear vision of the learning goals for your school and a plan for supporting teachers as they work toward those goals, and you have identified what kinds of tools and systems you need in place to make that happen, *then* you can focus on the specifics of funding: How much is it going to cost to make that vision possible?

I like to take an "If you build it, they will come" philosophy toward funding. Build out your plan—regardless of the reality of funding. Figure out how much funding you need to bring your vision to life. Once you have a plan, you know what to ask for. It's still surprising to me to see how many districts we work with find the money once they know what they want it for.

Build out your plan—regardless of the reality of funding. Once you have a plan, you know what to ask for.

Another tip: Look for hidden money. "I found money for our schools that was in flexible buckets," Jennie Magiera says. "A curriculum bucket can't always be used on devices, for example, but because we weren't spending a lot of money on paper or printer ink, I had money available in my supplies budget that could be used to buy devices. Be creative with your buckets, and don't subscribe to the idea that you have to have a minimum amount of money to bring devices into your classroom."

- *What is your dream budget? How much would you need to do everything you want in your school or district?*
- *Who could help you reach that funding goal?*
- *Where could funds be reallocated to better suit your school's or district's needs?*

Policy

Before we close out this chapter on building a robust infrastructure, I want to add a word on policy. Stephanie Shipton, the director of early engagement and strategic initiatives at Teach for America, introduced me to the phrase *policy infrastructure*. You'll hear more from Stephanie Shipton in the next chapter as we discuss the importance of engaged communities, but it is fitting to share some of her thoughts here about how policy supports, drives, or inhibits the effectiveness of technology in education. Like Mark Garrison, who focuses on lowering the barriers and

A Message from the Future

From: Tim Lee, Cofounder, Amplified IT,
@AmplifiedIT, AmplifiedIT.com

We need to go and think and act anew. Trying to do things like they've always been done is not going to work. We have to make sure that we understand that we're in this kind of new space, and we have to enable and provide the experiences for students in the K–12 space that we wouldn't have thought possible before . . . and be able to provide them access to technology, even if we aren't able to fully understand or control it.

making technology easy for teachers and students to use, Shipton believes that policy can do the same thing for district and school leaders. "Policy infrastructure can play such a critical and beautiful role in ensuring equity when done well," she says. "When you work inside an agency, there's potentially an opportunity to navigate the pathways so that you have a clear path for innovators to be able to move forward."

Those in leadership positions—the school board, superintendent, or building leaders—must work to create policies that clear the path for growth and innovation. And those who work within the system as educators must be conscious of the reality that policy is often more flexible than perception indicates. There's a myth in education that policy is rigid, and as a result, people may be afraid to try new things. But as Shipton points out, "Policies are really an opportunity for people to come together and, through relationships, make a difference with a shared vision and purpose." She shares the story of a principal in Hawaii who has turned his high school into a collection of small learning academies. "You now have students graduating from high school with their associate degree and with industry connections, having had apprenticeships and internship experiences," she says. "He did all that within the existing system on his own. He bootstrapped most of it and essentially hacked it so that his kids could have more opportunities."

The point is, policy has its place. It helps ensure equity. It sets basic boundaries and highlights opportunities. But it shouldn't prevent or inhibit learning experiences. Realizing that policy is often flexible empowers you—as a leader or a teacher—to step out of that cycle that keeps education from progressing and dare to try something new.

"Planning is an ongoing process and should include set times to review progress and revise the plan. Because technology changes rapidly, an annual review process is recommended. Consider scheduling the progress reviews to coincide with the district's budget process to ensure funding decisions are made with the latest information. Technology holds immense promise for education. Technology helps people learn, be creative, and become players and communicators in a global village. Technology, tied to the Internet, allows students of all ages to engage in knowledge building on a worldwide stage as never before possible."
–U.S. Department of Education, Technology Connections for School Improvement: Planners' Handbook

CHAPTER SEVEN
ENGAGED COMMUNITY

Change won't come from the top. Change will come from mobilized grassroots.
–President Barack Obama . . . in 1995

> ## Engaged community members understand what is possible in schools today, are included in the school vision, and are active in partnerships with the school.

If parents and other community members visit a school with the expectation of seeing children quietly lined up in rows, they might be put off when they see a cacophony of learning happening with students working in groups, moving around the space, and getting excited. Engaging communities is about updating expectations for what school can and should be. It's about getting buy-in so that when changes are made, devices go home, and staff and students start connecting and collaborating with people in the community—or around the globe—learning is supported by those outside the school's walls. Ideally, parents and community members can even be a driving force for change in schools once they share in the vision of what's possible. If teachers attend professional development at a conference or elsewhere, they can return to their school and pretend it never happened.

But if parents are included in the professional development that happens in a school community, you can't put that genie back in the bottle.

My first experience of intentionally engaging a community to get people on board with our change initiatives happened when I was contracted by Palm Springs Unified School District to help write an updated three- to five-year technology plan. Following the guide outlined by the state, we had developed a vision for the kind of learning we wanted to see in our schools. We had a plan for professional development, and we had identified the tools that would support that learning. As part of the effort to get stakeholders involved and funding approved, our schools hosted a series of events for parents where we shared our vision for what was possible for their kids. We painted a vision of their children connected to a world of learning:

- They're going to be able to connect with peers and experts around the world.

- They're going to be able to find a global and authentic audience for their work.

- They're going to be able to connect with the authors of the books they're reading.

We also gave parents the opportunity to offer feedback. At the time, which was around 2006, many of the parents were concerned about internet safety—an issue we addressed as we talked about digital citizenship and safety practices. Seeing the possibilities and hearing the advantages of technology helped replace their fears with excitement. By the end of each of those events, the parents walked away ready to see the new technology plan put into action.

Community engagement is important for a number of reasons, not the least of which is that parents, business leaders, and local politicians can all help drive positive change when they understand and are excited about what's possible in education today. In fact, community support is one of the most important factors to motivating the school board and superintendent at the district level and the school principal and teachers at the building level. If community members are fearful of or skeptical about using technology in schools or are apprehensive about tax increases to fund necessary purchases or upgrades, they may very well put up blockades to derail your plans. But if you can get the community interested in your change initiative, or if you can get the community excited about what's possible by showing them what other schools are already doing, that enthusiasm can help push education forward in your school or district. To do that, you have to open the doors to your school and invite people in—virtually and in person.

Community Galas

Like the events we hosted to highlight our district's technology plan in Palm Springs, community galas get people excited about what's going on in their local schools. Design consultant David Jakes encourages schools to launch initiatives and showcase their inspiring spaces—redesigned libraries and classrooms, makerspaces, and learning centers—with a celebration. Invite parents and community members in, feed them, and show off the new space and its capabilities. Hosting a community gala can also be a great way to engage the community in any new initiative at the school. Bring them in, share the vision, ask for their feedback or participation, and, most importantly, celebrate that it's happening in their community school.

> **Bring them in, share the vision, ask for their feedback or participation, and, most importantly, celebrate that it's happening in their community school.**

In my own child's school, I've seen how these events are effective in pushing for better learning opportunities for students. Families will come in to see the new space, and while they're there, they will see what other teachers are doing. Parents see, for example, how one fourth-grade teacher uses Minecraft EDU to craft cool projects for students. Aware, perhaps for the first time, of some of the interesting ways technology can be used in the classroom, the parents start asking questions and may ultimately demand that their own children get to have similar opportunities. Exposing parents and other community members to your school lets them see the potential—for education, technology, and learning spaces. And at the same time, these events provide the perfect opportunity to share your school's needs.

Communicate to Increase Involvement

Every school and every classroom has stories to share, projects to showcase, and wins to celebrate. So share those stories! And make sure your teachers and staff are sharing them as well. When something noteworthy happens in or for your school, make sure everyone in your community knows about it.

Communication through social media, blogs, Google Classroom notifications, email newsletters, and text messaging apps like Remind help increase parent involvement. Keeping school and classroom sites up to date (which can be done in some cases by students) keeps the doors open virtually between open houses and community galas. This is an opportunity for schools to tell their own story, on social media and in the mainstream media. Don't wait for something bad to happen for the school to be in the paper; share a press release when something exciting is launching or producing results.

Hands-On Sharing

Hands-on experiences are an excellent way to roll out new tech initiatives and make sure that devices are used properly—at school and at home. Monica Martinez, the executive director of global development for EdTechTeam, notes that while new tech is great, it needs to be strategically introduced. She shares the story of a district near Austin, Texas, that had received a large corporate grant for a one-to-one campaign. "Of course, the district was like, 'Yay, we're excited! But hold on. Every kid gets one, and then what do we do?'"

One part of the multipronged answer to that fortunate dilemma was to hold a Parent Day. On a Saturday, the district hosted an all-day event complete with food and big tents that served as session rooms. If parents wanted their children to get a device, they had to show up and participate in the sessions.

"The sessions focused on internet safety and digital citizenship. We answered questions like, What does it mean when my kid is on this device? What do I need to be aware of? How do I help protect my kid? How can I better support him at home? How can I help her with homework on this device?" Monica Martinez says. There were also sessions for the students so they could learn about the devices and how to use them responsibly. And at the end of the day, each student was able to take home a device. "The families got a lot out of the day, and it was great to hear a lot of parents say things like, 'We want more of this. We want to learn more, and we want to be able to help our children.'"

One-day events can be powerful, but communication is amplified through ongoing exposure to the school. Monica shares another story about the Parent and Child Time (PACT) program she was part of in Weslaco Independent School District, a low-socioeconomic community in South Texas. Monica worked to train parent liaisons, hired either on a full- or part-time basis by the district's individual schools, to conduct workshops at the schools. "The goal was simply to have parents and kids come in and do some fun activities and projects together using technology. We wanted to share with parents what's possible now and what's coming." The PACT sessions were a hit. "They went from having maybe twenty people to seventy-five or more, and the engagement and the amount of involvement from the community really grew."

Part of what made that involvement possible was that the school provided childcare for younger siblings to make it easier for parents to participate in the sessions. Additionally, the schools worked around parents' schedules by offering sessions at different times. Sometimes they were held during lunch hours or in the evenings. Other times, the workshops were held at a central location on the weekend where everyone, regardless of which school their children attended, could come in for hands-on exposure to what their kids were learning.

When parents couldn't come to the schools, the parent liaisons went to them. "In this particular area, you wouldn't find these devices in many homes, so the parent liaisons took an iPad with them to the child's house and did one-on-one, at-home training with the parents and their children," Monica says. It was just one more very powerful way to open the communication lines between the school and its families.

Learning Opportunities for Parents

Several unexpected positives came out of the PACT program Martinez headed up in Weslaco. One side effect of that training was that parents expected their kids to come home with assignments as cool as the activities Monica Martinez and the parent liaisons shared at the workshops. When that didn't happen, the parents asked the teachers about the iPads and the things they had learned at the workshops. In turn, the teachers asked the district for training so they could make the most of the devices in their classrooms. Of course, as noted in the previous chapter, that professional development should have happened to begin with, but because these parents were engaged and excited about the learning possibilities for their children, it happened—better late than never. Pressure from the parents caused the teachers to *want* the training, which is an important factor to successful professional development. (There's a huge difference in results when teachers *want* to be there rather than *have* to be there.) Ideally, the teachers in this district would have been engaged with the vision early on.

Another positive outcome of the PACT program was the learning that the parents experienced. "Aside from teaching parents about apps and tools that were great for the kids, the parent liaisons also started looking for ways to engage the parents and help them develop skills that are needed in the workplace, basic skills that could help them get better jobs," Martinez says. "They started using the iPad, for example, to help the parents learn English using apps like Duolingo. They even used some of the fun apps simply to allow parents to interact with different processes and develop some basic skills."

For this community, school engagement turned into true community engagement that empowered the adults as well as the children. By reaching out and providing learning opportunities for parents, the school worked in a very practical way to help close the equity gap. In turn, the parents pushed for more and better opportunities for their children.

Become a Technology Ambassador within Your School Community

What we've looked at so far in terms of engagement has to do with the external community—getting buy-in from people outside the school. That kind of engagement is vital. But if you are a tech coordinator or an early adopter of technology, you can play an important role in engaging and inspiring your internal school community to join the modern age and employ education technology in everyday situations.

Educators who love to try and test new gadgets and innovative technologies tend to race ahead of others in their schools, thereby increasing the equity gap instead of helping to close it. Conversely, Richard Culatta points out that there's also a risk of complacency for innovative educators to think that as long as other teachers in the building are moving slower by comparison in terms of integrating tech, they don't have to push harder to advance their teaching. "That's just not good enough for students," he says. "We all need to be constantly pushing what we can do, how we can improve, how we can use technology better."

One way tech-savvy educators can help push their schools into the future is to share what they're learning. "Be ambassadors for how to use tools in ways that are helpful for the other members of the school community," Richard advises. If you love cutting-edge technology and get excited about innovation, it's easy to get wrapped up in those things and forget to share them with others. Be intentional to share with your school community and your larger PLN what technology you're using and why. "Don't

GUEST VOICE: MONICA MARTINEZ
HOME, SCHOOL, AND COMMUNITY

Executive Director of Global Development, EdTechTeam,

@mimg1225,

Austin, Texas

We often hear, "It takes a village." To me, that village consists of home, school, and community. Without having those three, many people fall through the cracks, especially in low-socioeconomic areas where there are so many struggles. If one support fails, the other two can step in and pick up the slack.

I definitely had extensive home involvement. My mom, who became the director of the parental involvement program for Weslaco ISD, devoted her career to parental involvement, fought to make sure I learned English and Spanish—not the *Spanglish* that was used in our school's bilingual-ed program. (It was just a terrible program.) My grandmother taught us all how to play music, and through music we learned important skills that helped us further down the road.

The community aspect, for me, was really the church that my family belonged to because my great-grandfather, grandfather, and father were all ministers. There was a community of support there as well as a space to develop skills; those were the two really strong pieces in my life.

From school, I definitely had teachers who supported my creative side and gave me the space to flourish. All those three things coming together was really impactful and helped me succeed in a place where 50 percent of my class dropped out before graduation. I was lucky that I had all those three components in place to help me be successful, because I could have fallen into either 50 percent.

> I dream of a world where the lines between three different entities—home, community, and school—are blurred.

I dream of a world where the lines between three different entities—home, community, and school—are blurred. Where the home begins to embrace more of your education, and really begins to take ownership of the responsibility of a parent to play a part in the development, learning, and education of a child; where community becomes more open to allowing technology in schools; where schools do real-world projects that make an impact. It'd be great to see that kind of support for students.

A Message from the Future

I believe that if family, community, and school come together, it could truly change the landscape of opportunity, especially for your struggling learners.

GUEST VOICE: STEPHANIE SHIPTON
START WITH PEOPLE

Director, Early Engagement and Strategic Initiatives,

@slshipton, hawaii.teachforamerica.org,

Honolulu, Hawaii

Issues of equity and safety, such as Title IX for athletics and building codes, are areas where the Big-P policy, laws, and regulations can really play a strong role. We should always have some sort of building code standards, for example. There needs to be some level of strong, equitable foundation for safety and then access. Requiring that all kids go to school up to a certain age sets a baseline expectation. But Little-P policies, like assigning a certain number of instructional minutes that every student should have, goes too far.

So much of policy in education right now is trying to change culture. The idea is that if we just have a clear policy, for example, about attendance, we could change the behavior. We had a teacher here in Hawaii who wanted the school board to require that the principal of each school be responsible for taking attendance in every single classroom.

I think anybody who worked in a school knows that's not realistic. The teacher's reason for demanding that policy was there had been a student who left campus and got into an accident. That example sticks out to me because what the teacher was really trying to fix in that situation was not a process problem or a policy problem; it was a people and culture problem. You can't write policy to fix culture because culture is created by all of the things, spoken and unspoken, that each individual contributes to a space. To change culture, you have to start with people.

> ## You can't write policy to fix culture . . . . To change culture, you have to start with people.

I think that's why, often, folks are scared to do anything. There's a fear that if you do something to disrupt policies, then you're disrupting the whole system, and the other people who have a stake in it will be angry. I'm hopeful that will shift as we start to explore different models where it's not, for example, a union pitted against a department of education. That's where you have potential to create opportunity for people to come together over programs and initiatives. You also have the opportunity to use policy to elevate and add value to things that are important without diving too heavy handed into the details of how you get there.

A Message from the Future

With the way we engage each other and with the perceived and real rules of our system, if we could embrace our fear and lean into our empathy, we'd be at such a stronger starting place for conversations that could bring people together.

just talk about 'this new app' you've found; talk about a tough problem that teachers need to solve and show how it can be used as a tool to solve that problem," Richard says.

Engaging your colleagues and addressing real-life problems is a powerful way to change how they think about the way they use technology. So talk about how you use blogging and social media to build a powerful PLN, how you simplify parent communication with apps like Remind, and how you streamline with productivity and planning tools like G Suite. Being a technology ambassador is one simple action that any teacher or leader can take toward ensuring an equal-access environment for all students.

Engage the Community to Create Policies That Move *Society* Forward

As you open the doors to your school through in-person events and digital communication, consider how to involve community members in shaping the future of education. In Chapter Two, Nick Polyak pointed out that courageous leadership requires taking student and teacher voice into consideration when making decisions. Similarly, Michael Lubelfeld shared a story about how collaborative efforts between the district, business leaders, parents, and other community members made it possible to redesign twelve outdated science labs. "It was all done in an integrated approach through listening, leading, and learning," he said.

Collaboration isn't just a skill that we should help students develop for their future. Collaboration is a skill teachers and school leaders need to employ today—in both the daily operation of their schools and the more momentous decisions. Collaboration is the method we all must use if we are going to provide meaningful learning opportunities for today's students—opportunities that improve education and effect positive changes in our society.

"Our economy is shifting from an institution-based system to more of a sharing economy; there's a similar opportunity and change that needs to happen around the process for how we approach developing policies in education," Stephanie Shipton says. "It's a change and opportunity to be more inclusive and participatory, one that puts a premium and focus on equity and people."

Schools are not institutions that work in isolation; they are organizations that bring information, experience, wisdom, and people together to create and shape the future. Crafting policies collaboratively with people from across all strata of the community creates the conditions for great things to happen, ensuring equity and progress. That isn't always convenient or easy. The more voices in the room, the greater the odds are that there will be disagreements. But by the same token, the more diversity in the room, the greater the opportunity for growth and innovation. "From the school's standpoint, engagement requires being more daring and allowing for community involvement," Monica Martinez says.

So be daring. Be bold enough and *care* enough to engage your community. Share your vision for what's possible in education with parents, business leaders, and other community members. Strive to get buy-in by showing people what can be done—and how, through better learning opportunities, it's possible to drive education and society forward.

"Education is for improving the lives of others and for leaving your community and world better than you found it." **–Marian Wright Edelman, president and founder of the Children's Defense Fund**

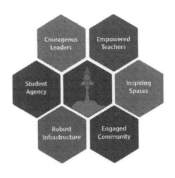

CHAPTER EIGHT
MORE *NOW*

The future is already here; it's just not very evenly distributed.

–William Gibson, novelist

You already know I'm a huge U2 fan. Since we opened *More Now* with an anecdote about the band, it seems a fitting way to wrap up the book and launch you into whatever comes next for you, your school, and your students. Aside from the band's musical talents, one of the reasons I like U2 so much is that the lyrics often hit home with me—making me think and inspiring me to imagine. "Dream out loud" is one of those lyrics, and it showed up in a few of U2's songs in the '90s. My favorite instance of that lyric is in a song called "Zooropa." The song, which is about the chaos in the world (especially with the ever increasing "advancement through technology"), opens with a mesh of techno sounds—sounds that aren't recognizable by their instruments. But as it comes to an end, Edge's guitar riffs clear through the techno-chaos, and you hear Bono singing over and over that, "She's gonna dream up the world she wants to live in; she's gonna dream out loud."

That's the mission I want you to take from this book: Dream up the world you want to live in, and empower those you work with and serve to do the same.

Today, more than ever, the world seems like it's in chaos, and some-times, technology seems to make life and education feel even more over-whelming. But bringing education forward and preparing students for the future takes more than just buying cool technology and putting it in classrooms. Devices, whether we're talking about Chomebooks, iPads, the Oculus Go, or students' own smartphones and tablets, are great. But if all we do is bring tech into classrooms without changing anything else, the learning experiences will have changed very little. Students will still be listening to teachers lecture, regurgitating notes, and completing online worksheets.

To prepare students for life today—and for all of our futures—we must look first to helping leaders, teachers, and students develop as people and as whole human beings.

Educational consultant Bernajean Porter once told me the story of a time when a priest in a school community she was working with com-plimented her for making educational technology planning (a typically dreary affair) a spiritual experience. I knew then I had a higher bar to aspire to in my work!

> To prepare students for life today
> —and for all of our futures—
> we must look first to helping leaders, teachers, and students develop as people and as whole human beings.

With that in mind, even as we look to the future and at the staggering possibilities technology offers in education (those that fill us with hope, and those that may fill us with dread), I believe we would do well to keep life in perspective. Looking back to ancient wisdom helps us remember our place in history. We can find inspiration from the various indigenous traditions upon which humanity's success has been built. A Celtic triad, for instance, suggests that many of our best insights come from an ancient place, which psychology and neural biology might support today: **"When** the soul is inspired, it inherits three gifts: primitive genius, primitive love, and primitive memory."

Here in the United States we can look to Native American wisdom for this inspiration. As the Chippewa Medicine Man known as Sun Bear said, "I do not think that the measure of a civilization is how tall its buildings of concrete are, but rather how well its people have learned to relate to their environment and fellow man."

While we help speed our students toward a future full of the promise of technology, we must also remember to help them to live in (and protect) a world of complex ecosystems that have evolved over millions of years and have supported human life for hundreds of thousands of years (many times longer than our recorded history), and to help them care for a world that will support human life for even longer to come. A similar sentiment is echoed in Australian Aboriginal wisdom as well: "We are all visitors to this time, this place. We are just passing through. Our purpose here is to observe, to learn, to grow, to love."

And as we help students develop as individuals, intellectually, emotionally, and spiritually—in their own ways, we must let them dream their own dreams of the future. As another Australian Aboriginal proverb says, "those who stop dreaming are lost." A Maori song from New Zealand captures the past, the future, and the importance of dreaming this way:

"Let us know you as you were in times gone by,

Let us know you as you are,

Let us know you as you dream you want to become."

I hope we will build schools that seek to know students in these ways too: In the context of the traditions they come from, in the reality of who they are when they come to school, and of course in the potential of who they can someday be. I always try to see people the way they want to be seen, and it serves me well. And it certainly supports the concept of student agency.

The Sámi of Northern Europe knew that "kindred spirits recognize each other." (The Welsh have a beautiful name for this concept of kindred spirits, *anam cara*, which roughly translates to "soul friend.") I hope we also create schools where kindred spirits of all ages can connect and find a sense of belonging, which modern psychology and organizational theory tells us is critical to any individual or team success, in academics and nearly any other endeavor in life. The Sámi are also known for a philosophy of **"work more and talk less."** These words of wisdom are an ancient yet still-relevant call for a focus on acting *now* to build on the past for a better future.

When brave and well-prepared educators dare to combine the wisdom of the past and the power of today's technology, we can push the limits of what education—and our students—can be. It's with that mindset that we can effectively promote student agency and community engagement so that everyone can see the amazing things our students can do *now*. And when we support the entire system with inspiring spaces and robust infrastructure, there's no limit to humanity's potential.

Each of the critical elements in the honeycomb has to be in place if we are going to see the needle move for school change. And if you can be the one who dreams out loud and then puts technology to work for your vision instead of being overwhelmed by it, you can help create the kind of world you want to live in—and the kind of world your students want to live in. Fortunately, many people and schools are leading the way and are already at work making their dreams become a reality. You can be one of them—or *continue* being one of them.

Start by Showing Others What's Possible

In Chapter Four, I shared with you some of the incredible and innovative work Brendan Brennan's team and students are doing at The Moonshot Laboratory in Hawaii. Students spend 20 percent of their learning time, one full day a week, in this leading-edge, technology-infused center where they collaborate with other students, teachers, and experts from around the world. The dream of the leaders for this innovative facility is that the students who work and learn there will become pillars in their communities, young people who could solve real problems and make a difference in the world—and for education as a whole. "Our hope is that because of their experiences at Moonshot Laboratory they will go back to their traditional schools and serve as agents of change—disruptors of traditional education," Brennan says.

Moonshot Laboratory was, at least partially, born out of frustration with a system that couldn't seem to get past the hurdles of how education has always been done. "We realized that as we were trying to work within the system to transform it, the system was really resistant to what we were trying to do. No matter how popular the professional development is, no matter how successful it is, no matter how much students' scores go up, there's always a resistance to change. Especially the change required to have students be at the center of innovation, at the center of problem-solving in their communities," he says.

Resistance in education often follows two main threads. The first is that teachers can't teach in ways that allow students to be truly innovative, that they don't have the necessary skills to support students in this kind of learning. The second idea is that students can't solve big, real-world problems or learn outside the traditional setting. And too often, those limiting ideas keep educators from trying new ways of working, teaching, and learning.

"We build these barriers around ourselves that we reinforce with our perceptions in the world," Brendan Brennan says. For the leaders at Moonshot Laboratory, the way around that resistance was to step outside the system and provide opportunities for students and educators to be inspired and empowered—to show people what's possible.

The way around that resistance was to step outside the system and provide opportunities for students and educators to be inspired and empowered—to show people what's possible.

GUEST VOICE: BRENDAN BRENNAN
WORKING OUTSIDE THE SYSTEM

Ground Control at Moonshot Incubator, Lead Education Architect, The Janus Group, @BrendanJanus, Honolulu, Hawaii

Earth-shaking transformations like Facebook and Microsoft were created by kids. Bill Gates and Mark Zuckerberg were going to the finest educational institution in the world, Harvard, as freshmen. They had to drop out to create real change in their communities in the world. That really says something. If the finest educational institution can't support the greatest thinkers, then we're doing something wrong.

We have a kid coming to Moonshot Laboratory who was at a regular school last year. He really likes basketball and had an idea for the science fair to create a glove that measures the distance, velocity, and angle to create the perfect free-throw shot. For the science fair, he made the poster and all the stuff about what the glove would do and how the gyroscope would measure velocity as well as angle based on the user's height and distance from the rim. But part of the science-fair requirements was a working prototype.

He said, "How can I build a working prototype? I don't have a gyroscope. I don't know how to code. I don't know how to build something like this." And he ended up getting a D on his science fair project even though the idea was sitting right there. He didn't have access to the resources necessary to build the prototype, so he earned a D.

This year, he came to the Moonshot Lab, where he has access to the tools. He has access to the training and the understanding. Now, he's building this thing and is on the way to creating his own company.

Standards-based education, bad teacher contracts, and bad legislators have kept us inside this box.

A Message from the Future

Students don't need to learn from us anymore. Learning is post-human. Learning math, learning the capitols, learning all this other stuff, it's post-human. Computers are going to be able to do it better than we do. They are going to be able to leverage that information, beat us, be better than we are at whatever it is.

What we're trying to focus on are those real, human characteristics that we need to push in education: collaboration, communication, creativity, and entrepreneurship. Those are the uniquely human traits that computers, we feel, will never be able to replicate, duplicate, or be better than us in accomplishing. The focus is not learning anymore; it's on nurturing the human traits that already exist in students. We have to ask, *How do we make sure those things flourish, grow, and become strong?* Because those are the only things they are going to have thirty years from now.

Kids take the lead at Moonshot Laboratory, but Brendan's team also puts a great deal of time into empowering educators so that what happens on his campus can happen elsewhere. One way they do that is by leading adults through an experience they call the Moonshot Growth Mindset Model. "We present adults with a challenge, and they'll openly say to us, 'That's impossible; we can't do that.' Then we scaffold them through actually accomplishing the impossible. When the adults see what they *can* accomplish, all of a sudden their thinking changes and they realize, 'Wow, we've been restraining these kids, and we've been restraining ourselves. We have been holding our kids back; our kids *can* do it.' In fact, not only can the kids do it, the kids can accomplish this 'impossible' task faster than the adults can."

When you consider all that children and teens have *already* accomplished, in terms of invention and innovation, the results are inspiring. The trampoline, the steam engine, the helicopter, earmuffs, the Braille system, the snowmobile, the list of things invented by people under twenty is incredible, and still, society says, "Kids can't do that."

"I think the misconception here is that these kids are the exceptions. I tend to think that they are the rule," Brennan says. He also notes that any of the young people who have created or innovated products "did so in spite of their archaic education institutions. They didn't do this while they were sitting in school; they did it sitting in a lab with all the tools, support, and other scientists and consultants."

The lesson here is that kids *can* do amazing things. *You* can do amazing things. If you're in a resistant community or school, start the shift toward progress by showing people what can be done. When in doubt, remember that sometimes it's necessary to be subversive. Don't be afraid to break the cycle and make a change you believe in. You can choose meaningful experiences and relationships over perpetuating an ineffective system.

Start with Technology

Another example of education pioneers who are turning dreams into reality is the team at Qneuro, a company that uses the latest technology to customize learning and, specifically, formative assessment. John Wick, the director of education at Qneuro, says the company's goal is to "make assessment more efficient, easier for everyone, and more accessible and fun for the students as well as the teachers and administrators who have to look at the data."

Using current education theory, neuroscience, and EEG devices, Qneuro's games assess common core math standards while personalizing the experience for the learner. During a tour of the Qneuro offices, Clark and Finn experienced games that could sense their flow state, their frustration, and their cognitive load, and adjust the challenges accordingly. They played simple concentration games as well as more complex games for teaching standards-based math content. In the "experimental" part of the office, they were fitted with highly accurate sensors that could tell where they were looking and where they were processing language.

John Wick explains how this cutting-edge use of technology works: "It looks at the brain waves that are coming through the headset and considers whether the student is being overtaxed in any number of channels. Is the visual complexity too high? Is the auditory channel too much? Is the learner getting excited? Is the student bored? As the student plays the game, the headset picks up on the cognitive load."

If the learner is having a hard time and the algorithm picks up the high cognitive load, the game will automatically adjust factors to improve the student's experience; for example, the visual complexity may decrease, removing nonessential imagery. That way, the student only sees the most important elements of the game—the assessment material or problems he or she needs to focus on. As the student learns and begins to complete the tasks more easily, the program notices a decreased cognitive load and brings the backgrounds back into focus so that the learner can play with the normal settings.

As a matter of privacy protection, neither teachers nor the folks at Qneuro see students' brain-wave activity. "All that the teacher sees is a report that shows whether the student is at, above, or below mastery or needs immediate intervention," Wick says. All adjustments to the difficulty of the game assessment happen behind the scenes, where algorithms adjust what the student sees and experiences based on how engaged, excited, or anxious the child is.

One of the most powerful aspects of Qneuro's games is the way they promote a growth mindset. When students fail to complete a task, they are encouraged to try again and again until they succeed. "As with most game applications, there are reward systems such as badges or things students can collect. Even if they have failed the math assessment five times, they *want* to take it again because they want to get those rewards," John Wick says. And because the game intensifies or decreases difficulty in real time based on how the student is responding, the learning experience is personalized and helps ensure mastery, not just completion.

"We're trying to build toward that growth mindset in everything we're doing," he says. "We're using modern technology the way it should be used to try to help kids. Rather than using worksheets and pencils and telling them to work from the book—1,500-year-old technology—to teach the skills that don't match the skills that they need for the world of tomorrow, let's actually start using modern technology tools—iPads and other devices—that they have and are already familiar with. Let's use those tools so students can learn and show what they know."

As games and the underlying AI improve, these sensors will be put to better and better use. Combining this technology with something like the Oculus Go, which the boys fell in love with just before this book went to print, and the natural human responses of the new Google Assistant, which was announced while I worked on the final edits of this book, makes the potential for ground-breaking virtual-learning environments with responsive AI tutors seem very real and very close at hand. It won't be long until we're less concerned with 1:1 implementations of Chromebooks or iPads, and we're more focused on helping educators work together

GUEST VOICE: JOHN WICK
ASSESSMENT FOR LEARNING

Director of Education, Qneuro, @JohnWick, TeacherWick.com,
Long Beach, California

Our game design comes from my own personal philosophy of education. I've always believed that when a kid fails a test, with rare exception, it's not the student's fault. It's usually because I, as the teacher, haven't found a way to reach the student yet. My own personal philosophy is that if my job title is *teacher*, then my job is to *teach* the material. I want that kid to be able to take an assessment as many times as possible, as many times as it takes to show me that they've learned the material.

Let's put it this way: When I went to high school, I failed algebra three times in a row. Outright, F, F, F. It was horrible. The last time I took it, the *fourth time*, I earned an A.

I wasn't allowed to give up, and eventually, I learned the material.

Why should we limit students? Let's allow them get to the point where they can update that assessment grade throughout the quarter. If they get a C- at the beginning of the quarter, let them take it again in a week. They may end up with an A+. Awesome!

A Message from the Future

Don't be afraid of trying the new technology; don't be afraid to take the steps to see if something that's coming up is better. Sometimes it will be. Sometimes it won't be.

You are an educator. You are a professional in this field. You have gone to advanced schooling to get the degrees and credentials you have. It's time we step away from just blindly accepting the textbooks that we're given and teaching from them as if that is the only way to teach. We have to step up and be the professionals that we're supposed to be. We must constantly evaluate what's out there and make sound pedagogical decisions based on what we have access to.

with technology very like the *Illustrated Primer* from Neal Stephenson's *Diamond Age* (a "book" with both AI tutoring and access to human tutors around the world when needed), or we're working remotely with students in fully virtual environments like those in Ernest Cline's *Ready Player One.*

Just Start!

Technology, when powered by science and wisdom, has a way of compressing the learning curve. The kind of learning that happened over the course of twelve grades one hundred years ago now happens far earlier in a student's education. And as my friend Michael Porcelli points out, "The eighteen-year-olds of tomorrow will probably be way smarter than you and I might ever be in our lifetimes." The plus side of the way technology allows us to learn, grow, and access information is that we can focus on powerful thinking tools, like understanding economic trade-offs or cognitive biases. "We can compress more of the key information, and let go of a lot of extraneous stuff," says Porcelli, who has been both a computer scientist at HP and the director of training at The Integral Center in Boulder, Colorado, where participants explore "the frontiers of what creates stronger relationships, minds, bodies, hearts, and lives." Technology also has the power to provide equitable, advanced learning experiences even in remote areas. "The mobile penetration in sub-Sahara Africa is skyrocketing; they're going to leapfrog over wire telephony entirely and probably wired internet as well," he predicts.

In a Google blog titled "The next billion users are the future of the internet," Caesar Sengupta, Google's vice president of the Next Billion Users Team, explains a few ways these leaps will play out for the next generation:

> Most of the next billion users have never used a PC and may never use one. They don't think of the internet as something you access with a mouse and a keyboard. A computer is not a terminal where you type in queries. A computer is a smartphone, and it also doubles up as a television, a wallet, a classroom, and a portal for government services.

GUEST VOICE: MICHAEL PORCELLI
SHIFT THE PARADIGM

Computer Scientist and Personal Transformation Coach,

facebook.com/michael.porcelli,

San Diego, California

Everyone is optimizing to hold your attention. Facebook doesn't care about your overall well-being, or even overall social well-being; they care about getting more money from ads. And if they keep you there longer, they can show you more ads. Their incentive is essentially building an algorithm that generates value for shareholders, and we—people plus the algorithms—are more like the product than the customer.

The question is, can we break out of that paradigm, or are we stuck in it? The answer, I think, actually has to do with issues like corporate governance and also issues with the way the finance industry, venture capital, and Wall Street work. Those are the factors which create these kinds of conditions of humans as products. If we let that same paradigm be the one that runs the education online artificial intelligence, that's bad. If that happens, we are essentially just programming better consumers rather than better citizens.

A Message from the Future

Your job, as an expert in knowledge and information, is about to be replaced by robots. You should not be afraid of that. Instead of being a source for knowledge and information, you should be a source of the kinds of things that humans can only get from other humans: friendship, mentorship, guidance, empathy, and what it takes to actually work together.

Your job, as a teacher, should be more like a mentor, a community leader, a mediator, an arbiter, potentially an exemplar of the whole person. Your job will become more like being a coach-therapist-mentor, but that's still a form of education. You're just educating certain facets of humanity that are the hardest for robots to replicate.

Because the breakthroughs that make ubiquitous comput-ing possible rely on cutting-edge work in artificial intelligence, we tend to think that advances will start in the most prosperous parts of the world and expand from there. But we've found with the Google Assistant, for example, that the next billion users adopt cut-ting-edge technology astonishingly quickly. Since we launched the Google Assistant on the first feature phone in December [2017], the Reliance JioPhones, usage of the Assistant in India has grown six times over the past four weeks. This isn't just due to many semi-lit-erate or illiterate users, but also the fact that typing is difficult for people who never grew up with a computer keyboard. The next bil-lion users will be the first to truly embrace ubiquitous computing, expecting apps to work in a natural way rather than having to learn all the artificial commands that we did on PCs.

The effect of those leaps in technological access advancement means that students anywhere—be it the wilds of Africa, rural towns in mid-dle America, or urban districts of Chicago or Los Angeles—can plug into information and incredible learning opportunities, even if their schools aren't. That's great, but it also means that we cannot afford to delay in mov-ing education forward. We must push for school change now because the future is already here. If we as educators and as a society fail to push for-ward, our students will move ahead without the guidance and support of someone who has the heart of an educator. We can't wait to dream; and we certainly can't wait to act.

More Soon

My emails often end with the sign-off, "more soon." I started using the phrase because I had this feeling of guilt over not having all the answers. I'd sign off "more soon," which, in my head, translated to, "I don't have all of the information I should have right now, but here's what I do have to share with you. More soon."

FUTURE-FOCUSED THOUGHTS FROM THE 2017 FOUNDER'S LETTER BY SERGEY BRIN

Just before this book went to print, the media reported on Sergey Brin's founder's letter. Some of the coverage seemed to suggest that Brin felt a mistrust of AI, but a close reading of the letter suggests that his reflections fall in line with the belief that we must hold on to our humanity even as we incorporate technology into our lives in exciting and even revolutionary ways.

Every month, there are stunning new applications and transformative new techniques. In this sense, we are truly in a technology renaissance, an exciting time where we can see applications across nearly every segment of modern society.

However, such powerful tools also bring with them new questions and responsibilities. How will they affect employment across different sectors? How can we understand what they are doing under the hood? What about measures of fairness? How might they manipulate people? Are they safe? . . . . There is serious thought and research going into all of these issues.

Even as we use technology in schools, we must validate the performance of these tools. We must teach media literacy and digital citizenship. We must ensure equitable access and allow our students and staff to use technology to share their voices.

Expectations about technology can differ significantly based on nationality, cultural background, and political affiliation. Therefore, Google must evolve its products with ever more care and thoughtfulness.

So should schools. Personalized, meaningful learning opportunities that provide real-life application will empower our students to lead the way for future generations. Education systems must evolve "with ever more care and thoughtfulness" if we are to meet the ever-expanding needs of our learners.

While I am optimistic about the potential to bring technology to bear on the greatest problems in the world, we are on a path that we must tread with deep responsibility, care, and humility.

Well said, Sergey.

When I first started collaborating with Jennie Magiera, she didn't read "more soon" the way I meant it. When she read it, she thought I was saying I wanted to hear from her *sooner*. As in, "Jennie, get back to me more quickly!"

We had a good laugh over the miscommunication, and much later, when she was offered a job at EdTechTeam, she sent me a two-word response: "More now."

But then I thought deeper about her focus on *more now*. There is a nugget of philosophy in those two words. It's the idea that we need to focus on the moment and be present. *More now* means looking less to yesterday—or even to tomorrow. It means giving up living in the past, holding onto the past, or feeling guilty about or constrained by it. *More now* also means less dreaming of the future and less talking about what could be (something that can be a bit difficult for people in our field). *More now* requires a focus on taking action, on moving things forward—right *now*. As fantasy author J.K. Rowling says, "It does not do to dwell on dreams and forget to live."

Throughout this book, you've seen so many powerful, future-focused messages from educators, leaders, and industry partners. Their words inspire in part because they come from people who are blazing trails right now. They don't have a crystal ball. They don't have all the answers. But they are taking action, moving forward, and happy to connect and collaborate with others as they forge ahead.

My own message from the future is this: Don't wait. Schools cannot be stagnant. They cannot look the way they did twenty years ago—or even five years or one year ago. Like Gibson says, the future is already here—and it's a moral imperative for educators to help distribute it more equitably. Don't wait until all the pieces are in place to make your move. You are an architect of the possible, and you can dream out loud today. This is only the beginning.

#MoreNow.

School change is never easy, and there is no "right" answer to the complex cultural and organizational challenges ahead.

At EdTechTeam, we believe meaningful school change requires a focus on Student Agency supported by Courageous Leaders, Empowered Teachers, Inspiring Spaces, Engaged Community, and Robust Infrastructure. Our experts can help your organization build capacity in each of these supporting elements.

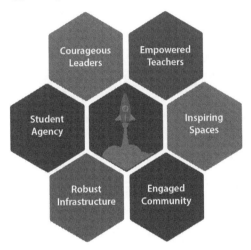

Our aim is to inspire and empower educators—to raise their awareness of what's possible, get them excited about their own vision, and help them feel confident that they can take the steps necessary to fulfill their goals. And this is only the beginning: EdTechTeam engages with schools as an active and responsive partner in long-term change initiatives.

EdTechTeam is a California Benefit corporation (and global network of educational technologists) founded by educators who are passionate about improving the world's schools using the best learning principles and technology available. Contact us for help transforming your school.

edtechteam.com/morenow

EDTECHTEAM VALUES

As a California Benefit Corporation, EdTechTeam is dedicated to improving education systems around the world. We've spent a lot of time learning about successfully innovative cultures, in schools, in Silicon Valley, and beyond. We've deliberately modeled our culture on those we admire, and hope sharing our model here might be helpful to others hoping to transform the culture in their own organizations.

VISION—The Future We Work Together to Build

EdTechTeam envisions a future where each student, regardless of background, becomes a compassionate and passionate global citizen working with others to solve meaningful problems while also having fun—and where education, access to technology, and a safe supportive environment makes this possible.

MISSION—The Role We Play In Service of Our Vision

We **inspire** and **empower** educators to **effect school change** using the best learning principles and technology available.

VALUES—How We Work Together in Service of Our Mission and Vision

We are **passionate** about our work, **flexible** in response to challenges, and **creative** in our solutions.

We seek **simplicity** over complexity, strive for **openness** with others, and embrace the **synchronicity** of "happy accidents and meaningful connections" in our work.

We work together best when living **healthy**, **balanced**, and **authentic** lives. We bring our whole selves to work, encourage others to do the same, and respect who they are.

We aim to improve **diversity**, **equity**, and **inclusion** on our team, at our events, and in our field.

We believe learning can be **fun**.

We are committed to **giving back** to the community of educators and students we serve.

In our efforts to exemplify these values, we **seek advice** from our teammates frequently, and we are brave and compassionate about **conflict resolution** focused on mutually beneficial solutions that serve our mission.

BIBLIOGRAPHY

Foreword

McLuhan, Marshall, Fiore, Q., and Agel, J. *The medium is the massage.* (New York: Bantam Books, 1967).

Chapter One

Brin, Sergey. "Why Google Glass?" TED Talk. February 2013, ted.com/talks/sergey_brin_why_google_glass. Accessed January 29, 2018.

"Vertigo." U2.com, September 14, 2005. u2.com/tour/date/id/4331.

Chapter Two

"May 25, 1961: JFK's Moon Shot Speech to Congress" *Space.com.* May 25, 2011. space.com/11772-president-kennedy-historic-speech-moon-space.html. Accessed March 5, 2018.

Wojcicki, Susan. "The Eight Pillars of Innovation." *Think with Google.* July 2011. thinkwithgoogle.com/marketing-resources/8-pillars-of-innovation. Accessed March 5, 2018.

Kounin, Jacob. *Discipline and Group Management in Classrooms.* (New York: Holt, Rinehart, and Winston, 1977).

"Google's ambitious Internet balloons soar above New Zealand." *CBSNews.com,* June 15, 2013, cbsnews.com/news/googles-ambitious-internet-balloons-soar-above-new-zealand.

enGauge 21st Century Skills: Literacy in the Digital Age. (Naperville, Illinois: North Ventral Regional Educational Laboratory, 2003).

Rushton Hurley, *Make Your School Something Special.* (EdTechTeam Press: Irvine, California, 2016).

Chapter Four

Papert, Seymour. "Hard Fun." papert.org/articles/HardFun.html. Accessed May 15, 2018.

Gee, James Paul. *What Video Games Have to Teach Us about Learning and Literacy.* (New York: St. Martin's Press, 2003).

Chapter Eight

Coyle, Daniel. *The Culture Code.* (New York: Bantam Books, 2018).

Sengupta, Caesar. "The next billion users are the future of the internet." *Google.* February 14, 2018. blog.google/perspectives/caesar-sengupta/next-billion-users-are-future-internet. Accessed May 9, 2018.

Brin, Sergey. "2017 Founder's Letter." *ABC Investor Relations.* abc.xyz/investor/founders-letters/2017/index.html. Accessed May 9, 2018.

ACKNOWLEDGMENTS

Like everything at EdTechTeam, this book was very much a team effort, and I could not have done it alone. I need to thank each of my friends and colleagues who appeared in the book, including Karen Cator, Jaime Casap, Richard Culatta, Richard Wells, Michael Lubelfeld, Nick Polyak, Chris Lehmann, Heather Dowd, Sarah Thomas, Wendy Gorton, Kevin Brookhouser, Trevor MacKenzie, Brendan Brennan, David Jakes, Rebecca Hare, Mark Garrison, Jennie Magiera, Tim Lee, Peter Henrie, Monica Martinez, Stephanie Shipton, Michael Porcelli, and John Wick. Thank you for spending time with me during our interviews (I was grateful for the chance to chat!), and thank you for your generous contributions to this book. Thank you also to Rushton Hurley and Ron Starker for the excerpts they contributed. And thank you to James Sanders for his early work inspiring and defining the honeycomb.

Thank you to MaynRad Brenes and Genesis Kohler for their work on the cover. And a special thank you to my son, Finn, for his patience (mostly) during the photo shoot at the EdTechTeam office.

A very special thank you is owed to Erin Casey, who has been a key part of so many books published by EdTechTeam Press, and who played an even bigger role in managing this project and seeing it through to fruition. It is a pleasure working with you, Erin.

Thank you also to Holly Clark, Director of EdTechTeam Press, for growing our publishing arm from nothing, for making this opportunity possible for me, and for supporting me at every step of the process.

I owe a debt of gratitude to everyone who works with me at EdTechTeam. This book, all the work we do, and all the learning I experience in schools around the world would not be possible without the team. I'm grateful to all forty of our employees, to the hundreds of practicing educators we hire each year, and to the thousands of others who step up and present or share with their peers at our events. I need to acknowledge individually those who have been on this journey with me the longest and given so much of their lives to this effort. Thank you, Chris Bell, Molly Schroeder, Michael Wacker, Wendy Gorton, and Jim Sill. You are all family to me.

And, of course, none of this would be possible without the understanding, flexibility, and support of my family at home—my wife Eva and our boys, Clark and Finn.

More from EdTechTeam Press
EdTechTeam.com/books

The HyperDoc Handbook: Digital Lesson Design Using Google Apps
By Lisa Highfill, Kelly Hilton, and Sarah Landis

The HyperDoc Handbook is a practical reference guide for all K–12 educators who want to transform their teaching into blended-learning environments. The HyperDoc Handbook is a bestselling book that strikes the perfect balance between pedagogy and how-to tips while also providing ready-to-use lesson plans to get you started with HyperDocs right away.

The Google Infused Classroom: A Guidebook to Making Thinking Visible and Amplifying Student Voice
By Holly Clark and Tanya Avrith

This beautifully designed book offers guidance on using technology to design instruction that allows students to show their thinking, demonstrate their learning, and share their work (and voices!) with authentic audiences. *The Google Infused Classroom* will equip you to empower your students to use technology in meaningful ways that prepare them for the future.

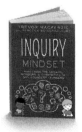

Inquiry Mindset: Nurturing the Dreams, Wonders, and Curiosities of Our Youngest Learners
By Trevor MacKenzie and Rebecca Bathurst-Hunt

Inquiry Mindset offers a highly accessible journey through inquiry in the younger years. Learn how to empower your students, increase engagement, and accelerate learning by harnessing the power of curiosity. With practical examples and a step-by-step guide to inquiry, Trevor MacKenzie and Rebecca Bathurst-Hunt make inquiry-based learning simple.

Dive into Inquiry: Amplify Learning and Empower Student Voice
By Trevor MacKenzie

Dive into Inquiry beautifully marries the voice and choice of inquiry with the structure and support required to optimize learning. With Dive into Inquiry you'll gain an understanding of how to best support your learners as they shift from a traditional learning model into the inquiry classroom where student agency is fostered and celebrated each and every day.

Innovate with iPad: Lessons to Transform Learning
By Karen Lirenman and Kristen Wideen

Written by two primary teachers, this book provides a complete selection of clearly explained, engaging, open-ended lessons to change the way you use iPad with students at home or in the classroom. It features downloadable task cards, student-created examples, and extension ideas to use with your students. Whether you have access to one iPad for your entire class or one for each student, these lessons will help you transform learning in your classroom.

The Space: A Guide for Educators
By Rebecca Louise Hare and Robert Dillon

The Space supports the conversation around revolution happening in education today concerning the reshaping of school spaces. This book goes well beyond the ideas for learning-space design that focuses on Pinterest-perfect classrooms and instead discusses real and practical ways to design learning spaces that support and drive learning.

Classroom Management in the Digital Age: Effective Practices for Technology-Rich Learning Spaces
By Patrick Green and Heather Dowd

Classroom Management in the Digital Age guides and supports teachers through the new landscape of device-rich classrooms. It provides practical strategies to novice and expert educators alike who want to maximize learning and minimize distraction. Learn how to keep up with the times while limiting time wasters and senseless screen-staring time.

The Google Apps Guidebook: Lessons, Activities, and Projects Created by Students for Teachers
By Kern Kelley and the Tech Sherpas

The Google Apps Guidebook is filled with great ideas for the classroom from the voice of the students themselves. Each chapter introduces an engaging project that teaches students (and teachers) how to use one of Google's powerful tools. Projects are differentiated for a variety of age ranges and can be adapted for most content areas.

Sketchnotes for Educators: 100 Inspiring Illustrations for Lifelong Learners
By Sylvia Duckworth

Sketchnotes for Educators contains 100 of Sylvia Duckworth's most popular sketchnotes, with links to the original downloads that can be used in class or shared with colleagues. Interspersed throughout the book are reflections from Sylvia about what motivated her to create the drawings as well as commentary from many of the educators whose work inspired her sketchnotes.

Code in Every Class: How All Educators Can Teach Programming
By Kevin Brookhouser and Ria Megnin

In *Code in Every Class*, Kevin Brookhouser and Ria Megnin explain why computer science is critical to your students' future success. With lesson ideas and step-by-step instruction, they show you how to take tech education into your own hands and open a world of opportunities to your students. And here's the best news: You don't have to be a computer genius to teach the basics of coding.

Making Your School Something Special: Enhance Learning, Build Confidence, and Foster Success at Every Level
By Rushton Hurley

In *Making Your School Something Special*, educator and international speaker Rushton Hurley explores the mindsets, activities, and technology that make for great learning. You'll learn how to create strong learning activities and make your school a place where students and teachers alike want to be—because it's where they feel energized, inspired and special.

The Google Cardboard Book: Explore, Engage, and Educate with Virtual Reality
An EdTechTeam Collaboration

In *The Google Cardboard Book*, EdTechTeam trainers and leaders offer step-by-step instructions on how to use virtual reality technology in your classroom—no matter what subject you teach. You'll learn what tools you need (and how affordable they can be), which apps to start with, and how to view, capture, and share 360° videos and images.

Transforming Libraries: A Toolkit for Innovators, Makers, and Seekers
By Ron Starker

In the Digital Age, it's more important than ever for libraries to evolve into gathering points for collaboration, spaces for innovation, and places where authentic learning occurs. In *Transforming Libraries*, Ron Starker reveals ways to make libraries makerspaces, innovation centers, community commons, and learning design studios that engage multiple forms of intelligence.

Intention: Critical Creativity in the Classroom
By Amy Burvall and Dan Ryder

Inspiring and exploring creativity opens pathways for students to use creative expression to demonstrate content knowledge, critical thinking, and the problem solving that will serve them best no matter what their futures may bring. Intention offers a collection of ideas, activities, and reasons for bringing creativity to every lesson.

Making Your Teaching Something Special: 50 Simple Ways to Become a Better Teacher
By Rushton Hurley

In the second book in his series, Rushton Hurley highlights key areas of teaching that play a part in shaping your success as an educator. Whether you are finding your way as a brand new teacher or are a seasoned teacher who is looking for some powerful ideas, this book offers inspiration and practical advice to help you make this year your best yet.

The Conference Companion: Sketchnotes, Doodles, and Creative Play for Teaching and Learning
By Becky Green

Wherever you are learning, whatever your doodle comfort level, this jovial notebook is your buddy. Sketchnotes, doodles, and creative play await both you and your students. Part workshop, part journal, and part sketchbook, these simple and light-hearted scaffolds and lessons will transform your listening and learning experiences while providing creative inspiration for your classroom.

Bring the World to Your Classroom: Using Google Geo Tools
By Kelly Kermode and Kim Randall

We live and work in a global society, but many students have only a very small community or neighborhood as their frame of reference. Expand their horizons and help them increase their understanding of how they fit in the global landscape using Google Geo Tools. This book is packed full of how-tos and sample projects to get you and your learners moving forward with mapping, exploring, and making connections to the world around you.

50 Ways to Use YouTube in the Classroom
By Patrick Green

Your students are already accessing YouTube, so why not meet them where they are as consumers of information? By using the tools they choose, you can maximize their understanding in ways that matter. *50 Ways to Use YouTube in the Classroom* is an accessible guide that will improve your teaching, your students' learning, and your classroom culture.

Illuminate: Technology Enhanced Learning
By Bethany Petty

In *Illuminate*, author, educator, and technology trainer Bethany Petty explains how to use technology to improve your students' learning experiences. You'll learn specific how-tos for using a wide variety of apps and tools as well as the why behind using technology. Meet your students' needs and make learning memorable using technology enhanced learning.

The Martians in Your Classroom: STEM in Every Learning Space
By Rachael Mann and Stephen Sandford

In *The Martians in Your Classroom*, educator Rachael Mann and former Director of Space Technology Exploration at NASA Stephen Sandford reveal the urgent need for science, technology, engineering, and math (STEM) and career and technical education (CTE) in every learning space. Proposing an international endeavor to stimulate students' interest in science and technology, they highlight the important roles educators, business leaders, and politicians can play in advancing STEM in schools.

ABOUT THE AUTHOR

Formerly a high school English teacher, Mark Wagner has since served as an educational technology coordinator at the site, district, and county levels. He now serves as President and CEO of the EdTechTeam, a global network of educational technologists that provides professional development and consulting services to learning institutions, nonprofits, and for-profit education companies. The EdTechTeam is a California Benefit Corporation with a mission to improve the world's education systems using the best technology and pedagogy available. They aim to inspire and empower other educators to do the same.

Mark Wagner has a PhD in Educational Technology and a master's degree in cross-cultural education. His doctoral research focused on the use of video games in education, and specifically on the potential applications of massively multiplayer online role-playing games (MMORPGs) as constructivist learning environments.

Outside of his work, Mark loves playing hockey, practicing martial arts, and obsessing over electric cars . . . and his '62 Beetle. He enjoys songwriting, spending time in nature, and exploring the world with his friends and family. He lives in Irvine, California, with his wife, Eva, and boys Clark and Finn. Naturally, he's a U2 fan.

52497711R00096

Made in the USA
Columbia, SC
04 March 2019